Good Practice Guide: **Starting a Practice**

RIBA Good Practice Guides

Other titles in this series:

Negotiating the Planning Maze, by John Collins and Philip Moren (2006)

Keeping Out of Trouble, by Owen Luder, 3rd edition (2006)

Employment, by Brian Gegg and David Sharp (2006)

Good Practice Guide:
Starting a Practice

A Plan of Work

Simon Foxell, The Architects Practice

RIBA Publishing

Published by RIBA Publishing, 15 Bonhill Street, London EC2P 2EA

ISBN-10 1 85946 249 9
ISBN-13 978 1 85946 249 2

Stock Code 59233

British Library Cataloguing in Publications Data
A catalogue record for this book is available from the British Library.

Publisher: Steven Cross
Commissioning Editor: John Elkington
Project Editor: Anna Walters
Editor: Alasdair Deas
Designed by Ben Millbank
Typeset by Academic + Technical, Bristol
Printed and bound by Hobbs the Printer, Hampshire

RIBA Publishing is part of RIBA Enterprises Ltd.
www.ribaenterprises.com

Series foreword

The *RIBA Good Practice Guide* series has been specifically developed to provide architects, and other construction professionals, with practical advice and guidance on a range of topics that affect them, and the management of their business, on a day-to-day basis.

All of the guides in the series are written in an easy-to-read, straightforward style. The guides are not meant to be definitive texts on the particular subject in question, but each guide will be the reader's first point of reference, offering them a quick overview of the key points and then providing them with a 'route map' for finding further, more detailed information. Where appropriate, checklists, tables, diagrams and case studies will be included to aid ease of use.

RIBA Good Practice Guide: Starting a Practice

Despite being a completely new book, this guide follows in the footsteps of previous RIBA guides to starting a practice, including *Starting up in Practice* (first edition 1987), written by a group under my chairmanship, and *A Guide to Starting a Practice* (first edition 1999), edited by Ramona Khambatta and published as part of RIBA Publications' Small Practices series.

The advice offered then still largely holds good today, although advances in technology and ICT have transformed many of the working tools and environments of architects in the interim. The foreword of the 1987 guide states 'Starting a practice, especially from scratch, is not for the fainthearted', and that is as true today as it was then.

This guide covers a large number of areas relevant to those thinking of starting a practice, but it is far from comprehensive and no substitute for obtaining good hands-on advice and expert assistance. There are also many other sources of advice to be consulted, some specifically about the business of architecture and many others about business matters generally. Use them in conjunction with this volume.

Whether you are thinking about starting a practice or you have already taken the plunge, then read this excellent and thorough guide. Running your own practice may not be for everyone and it can deliver a bumpy ride, but it can also bring great rewards and satisfactions. I do not regret for a moment starting and running my own practice over 30 years ago and it has proved very successful in many different ways. I am looking forward to seeing many more firms emerging and flourishing in the future and the guidance in the following pages will considerably help them to do so.

Jack Pringle
President, RIBA

Preface

Why are you reading this guide? Thank you for buying a copy, but you shouldn't even be thinking about starting your own practice.

Almost everyone who has considered the prospects for the architectural profession in the UK and beyond in recent times has concluded that the future, at least in the short and medium term, will belong to those with the financial and organisational muscle to secure work from similarly large-scale client bodies and groups. They generally agree that those commissioning buildings are now, and will be for the foreseeable future, looking for building designers who can deliver quickly, efficiently, economically and reliably: designers who know their way around the construction and property industries and are able to work directly with other members of the supply chain on an equal footing. Clients will be looking for 'safe pairs of hands', who are a 'fit' with their own outlook and have a track record of delivery.

If you are ambitious and talented you should logically work for an organisation that will give you the opportunity to design some of the biggest and most exciting projects around, with the backup and firepower that you will need to make your mark. Unsurprisingly, you are also likely to be better paid in such an organisation. Most other professions think this way: academics want to work in the best and most prestigious universities, doctors in the top hospitals, engineers for the big global consultancies. But not architects – over half the architects (54 per cent) surveyed in 2002 were principals in private practice, and just under half of those (23 per cent) were sole practitioners.

The notion of the celebrity, hypercreative and globetrotting architect has become ubiquitous, and has eclipsed the existence of the well-staffed office working in fame's shadow. Maybe this has fired up a profession already romantically wedded to the idea of the small creative studio or atelier to believe that the only way of 'making it' is to do so in their own name on the back of their individual genius.

Don't do it. There are already too many small practices out there, including mine, surviving on a proportionately very small part of the construction spend in the UK and beyond. But if you do, then certainly read this guide first. It will not tell you how to design; it assumes that you know how to do that already, and this will be the last mention of building regulations and door schedules. Its subject is running a business as an architect. In a deregulated and computer-enabled world this is no longer so different from managing many other service-driven, ideas businesses, especially in the 'creative economy' sector. But it is not an activity architects are educated for, despite being essential, and it can feel like a strange and hostile world.

Starting a practice should be approached with all the seriousness and enjoyment of a design project, and in that spirit the chapters are arranged in the form of the *RIBA Plan of Work*: taking the idea from inception and feasibility through to post-occupancy evaluation. And, just like a building, you really shouldn't start a practice until you've got a very good idea of what it is for, what it is going to be made of and how it will work.

I started my own practice twenty years ago. It was a straightforward affair, beginning with one day a week (plus evenings and weekends), and involved picking up jobs via contacts, working to a standard fee scale and not worrying about things such as business plans, cash flow or professional indemnity insurance. I had a drawing board and a typewriter, and although I rapidly bought one of the first rudimentary consumer-level computers I did not need much more. A lot has changed since then to make it a much more complicated affair, although even more practices seem to be set up today than ever – many blossoming briefly and then disappearing, leaving only the more robust and canny in their wake.

This guide is the result of those twenty years; years spent making a practice work – largely by trial and error. Years spent observing and discussing with my peers how they do it and, in more recent years, spent researching and writing on professional issues and organising events and conferences to throw light on, among other subjects, procurement, running small architectural practices and the role of architects in cities and society.

I do not claim to run a more successful or higher achieving practice than anyone else – almost certainly the reverse is true. The advice given in this guide is very much in the spirit of 'don't do what I do, do what I say'. It is borne out of experience and observation, but it has no magic recipe for success – running a business is a creative activity and does not work to a pre-set formula. The guide is here to be used: to suggest other ways of doing things, ways that may not always feel immediately comfortable, to remind you of what may seem to be blindingly obvious and to provide companionship and support. I hope that it will help you think about why you want to set up a practice and, if you really insist, how you might go about it and, ultimately, succeed at a difficult game in a tough world.

Simon Foxell
May 2006

About the author

Simon Foxell is an architect and principal of The Architects Practice, based in North London. He was an RIBA Council member from 1999 to 2005 and has been a main Board Director of the RIBA. He has chaired various RIBA committees, including Small Practice, Policy and Strategy and London region.

He established The Architects Practice in 1986 and has remained its principal ever since. The practice works predominantly in the residential, commercial and education sectors and the results have been widely published.

Simon Foxell is the editor of *The professional's choice – the future of the built environment professions* (Building Futures, 2004) and several policy and guidance documents for the RIBA and CABE. He is a CABE Enabler and RIBA-accredited Client Design Advisor.

Acknowledgements

This guide could not have been written without the many clients of The Architects Practice, whom, for the past twenty years, have allowed me to practise on them in an attempt to work out how to do the business of architecture successfully. Thanks are due to them all for their forbearance and understanding. This guide is dedicated to them, and especially to the great majority who have willingly come back for repeat treatment.

Substantial thanks are also due to the many who have helped directly in the writing of this book. Richard Brindley, Director of Practice at the RIBA, John Elkington at RIBA Enterprises and Alasdair Deas have offered essential support. Elspeth Clements of Clements and Porter Architects, Oliver Smith of 5th Studio, Robert Sakula of Ash Sakula Architects, David Lovegrove of Format Milton Architects, Charlie Hussey of Sutherland Hussey Architects and Andrew Kirby of ARK Projects all read the first draft of the text and came back with many useful insights, comments and suggestions, many of which have been incorporated into the guide. I am very grateful to all of them, particularly when I have failed to get back to them within a reasonable time. Responsibility for the final version of the text, however, remains with me.

Finally, thanks are owed to all my family, who have had to live with both an architect and an author, when I could have chosen far more straightforward ways of earning a living. The house will be finished soon – I promise.

Simon Foxell
August 2006

Contents

Work Stage A
Appraisal and feasibility

At the point when you are considering starting a practice you need to do a basic appraisal of your options and opportunities. What are your motivations and what are your chances of making it a success? How will it affect your income, lifestyle and ambitions? Can you afford it and is this the optimum time?

This will be the first iteration of business financial model.

Why?

Inevitably, given the challenges, the crowded nature of the field and the low financial rewards, even for those who succeed in other ways, the first question you need to be able to answer when considering setting up your own practice is 'Why?'

There are three main reasons for starting a new business in the UK: redundancy, the desire to make money for yourself and the freedom that can result from being your own boss. It is probably only the last of these that is a significant motivator for architects, although the freedom in question may be more one of expression than of the search for a relaxed lifestyle. Assess your motivations, in part to find out if you seriously want to take the idea further, but also to make sure the firm you plan to start fulfils your ambitions.

There are many ways for architects to work and make careers using their interesting and unusual set of skills. Running an architectural practice is only one of them – even if the training focuses most architects' ambitions narrowly onto it – and is the almost conventional response of many architects in their thirties who decide to strike out on their own. The result is the establishment of large numbers of lookalike practices, which by and large base their offers of services around the schedules in the standard forms of appointment. Why, as a creative person or group, would you want to follow them? Consider taking a more pioneering approach and developing your business around your enthusiasms and particular skills, and see if you can spot and fill any gaps in the market for your services. The most successful firms are those which have chosen to be entrepreneurial and have a distinctive and maybe unique quality that marks them out. Why not join those instead?

What?

What are your ambitions? What is it that you want to achieve and by when? Practices that have survived into maturity tend to have gone through a series of phases, often starting with private domestic work, competition entries or projects for family and other relations, and often building more in the way of credibility than significant construction projects. Only in later phases are they likely to be working on the type of projects that had inspired them to start up in the first place.

Famously in the 1950s, while still at university, the conservative politician Michael Heseltine mapped out his future career on the back of an envelope – *1950s: millionaire; 1960s: MP; 1970s: minister; 1980s: cabinet; 1990s: Downing Street* – only getting the last decade wrong (he made it as far as Deputy Prime Minister). Do something similar, in order to establish what it is that you want to have accomplished by a number of key dates and to decide on the best vehicle to get you there.

You may have had offers of work already and this has become the driver persuading you to launch a new business. The opportunity may well be too good to miss, although there may be other ways of handling it, including offering the project to your current employer. Look beyond such opportunities and examine the chances for establishing a practice based on the work that you really want to do and that you are confident that you can win in future.

Who?

Do you already know who you will be starting the practice with? Is it more a matter of friends wanting to work together, or have you already assessed how your skills, personalities and experience might complement each other to form a useful team and planned the practice on that basis? Have you tested how well you can work together? Life partners may want to be work partners as well, but can their relationship withstand being together nearly 24 hours a day. Friendships that work because of similarity may not provide the range and variety of approaches needed to succeed in a work environment. If you have not already worked as a team, consider doing something testing together, for example a voluntary project or a survival training weekend, to see how you get on when you really need to rely on one another.

The question of 'Who?' may do more to define the nature of your practice than any other. Appraise your approach to this issue with all the rigour it demands. Do not just stumble into it simply because it 'feels right' at the time.

Team roles/team building

The different roles required to successfully take a project from inception to completion have inevitably been the subject of considerable academic study and prognostication.

Two of the better-known categorisations are the Belbin Team Roles, based on Dr Meredith Belbin's work at Henley Management College, and the Management Team Roles indicator (MTR-i), associated with Myers–Briggs personality types:

Belbin

- Plant (creative problem solver)
- Co-ordinator
- Monitor evaluator
- Implementer
- Completer finisher
- Resource investigator
- Shaper
- Teamworker
- Specialist
  (see www.belbin.com)

MTR-i

- Coach
- Crusader
- Explorer
- Innovator
- Sculptor
- Curator
- Conductor
- Scientist
  (see www.teamtechnology.co.uk)

American attorneys have distilled all this into a much simpler categorisation:

- Finders: those who generate new business
- Minders: those who manage and look after both projects and existing clients
- Grinders: those who do the real work

You will need to have or be all three.

When?

Even when you know that you want to start up a new practice, timing is still essential. Is it a good moment in your career(s)? Have you accumulated the right level of experience, know-how, contacts and financial means? Are your families able to support you financially and emotionally at this point in their lives or are other events going to intervene or command resources and attention? Is the financial climate conducive to new businesses entering the market? Might you not be better off giving more time to the planning and developing of all aspects of the proposed new business prior to its launch?

It is more than likely for you to feel that the timing is out of your hands, and that a combination of opportunity, situation, age, general circumstance and impatience make this the required or the ideal moment. But even then, try to control the timing as far as you are able, if necessary by taking alternative short-term work until you are ready. Do not be rushed into starting up your practice, if only because it takes a lot of preparation and planning to get it right.

Feasibility study

Having asked the big questions, you will need to progress onto a more detailed feasibility assessment to see if setting up a business, whether on your own or with others, is something that you want to pursue and take further. On the assumption you want your new venture to last into the foreseeable future, the three tests are those of the triple bottom line of sustainability: economic, social and environmental.

Your appetite for dealing with all these issues and coming out on top should help you to decide whether starting on your own is for you. You may reasonably prefer to stay in an established firm, among like-minded colleagues and on a career track that could take you to a partnership/directorship within a relatively few years.

Also consider the type of work you want to do. The current economic and procurement climate is such that most large and medium-sized projects will go to the larger practices and to those with a lengthy track record; this includes the great majority of public sector work. There is still a good living to be made from the remaining range of projects, but the overall diet is inevitably thinner and may not always offer the same type of job satisfaction. If you wish to work on significant projects, including in the commercial, health and education

Feasibility tests – economic issues

Look at a timescale of five years from the start of your practice and consider the following questions:

What will you sell?

- Although architects pride themselves on happily taking on almost any project from a new spoon to a new town, in practice the mixture between what you want to do and what clients are likely to commission you to do is far more restricted. Make a broad assumption on the type and size of work you are likely to win each year, as the practice develops and matures, and match it to the likely timescale and your capacity for delivering each project. This may result in only a handful of profitable projects. Ensure you allow enough of the principals' time for running the practice, marketing and doing speculative projects, such as competitions and fee bids. Will you do anything else to supplement your fee income? Many young practitioners teach, and sub-contract work may be available from other practices.

- If you already have commissions or the chance of them you can usefully apply a probability factor to your income forecast (1.0 if you've got the job, 0.33 if you're one of three on a shortlist, etc.) – over a number of jobs this can add up to a surprisingly accurate forecast.

Add up the likely fees and income for each year (A).

Who will be doing the work?

- Make an assessment of how many people you will have working to deliver your projected workload. Include any partners or directors in your assessment.
- Magazines such as *Building* (www.building.co.uk) publish regular surveys of staff costs.
- See www.hmrc.gov.uk/calcs/nice.htm for a National Insurance contributions calculator.

Add up the salaries for each year plus any National Insurance costs (B).

Continued

Where will you work?

- Do you need premises, or will you work from home?

If you will be renting accommodation then make an assessment of your rent for each year, or if you already have premises, calculate the rent you will lose not letting it out to others (C).

What will your overheads be?

- Make some reasonable guesses for the following:
  - utility bills (heating, electricity, water, phones, internet connection, etc.)
  - business rates
  - professional fees (accountants, lawyers, PR, etc.)
  - membership fees (ARB, RIBA – both individual and practice, etc.)
  - marketing budget
  - premises costs (including cleaning, repairs, redecoration, etc.)
  - equipment and materials costs (including computers and other equipment as well as software and consumables)
  - leased services (including subscriptions to journals, a library service, etc.)
  - transport costs (including vehicle depreciation, fuel, servicing and tax)
  - property, contents and public liability insurance
  - professional indemnity insurance
  - bank charges and interest payments.

Add up your overheads (D).

Your economic assessment

For each year compare your income, (A), with the sum of your outgoings, (B) + (C) + (D), and see how soon you can break even and whether profit begins to build up over time. You will undoubtedly want to play with these figures so use a spreadsheet to adjust them, but do not be tempted to make them overly favourable as some large sums are likely to have been left out along the way. Aim for at least a 15 per cent profit to allow for fluctuations. Compare your potential income with getting paid employment elsewhere. Do a similar exercise with the benefits you are likely to gain in employment versus self-employment.

Continued

Starting a practice is not for the faint-hearted and the aim of the above exercise is to ensure you are investigating it with your eyes wide open. The income of most small practice principals is derisory at an average of approximately £35,000 per annum. Many inevitably earn considerably less than that.

The figures you have developed are likely to highlight a need for some form of investment, even if it is only an overdraft facility to tide you over periods of negative cash flow. If it is any more than the barest minimum, you will need to consider where the investment will come from. You may have enough yourself to invest or be able to extend your mortgage(s), or family and friends might be willing to lend you start-up capital, but the likelihood is that you will need to borrow it at a commercial rate of return from a bank or other financial institution. If so, it is more than likely that they will look for some form of collateral, possibly in the form of a charge on your house(s). Ensure that you can either afford the investment yourself or that you know and are willing to accept the risk to your property if your business venture does not succeed in the way you planned.

Feasibility tests – social issues

Consider the following sets of questions:

For the one-person practice/sole proprietor

- How are you on your own?
  - Do you get lonely or stir-crazy?
  - Do you have support and backup from friends/family/colleagues?
  - Are you self-willed and disciplined?
  - Do you indulge in displacement activity/can you deal with distractions?
  - Can you multitask?
  - Are you multiskilled (as a salesperson + designer + administrator, etc.)?
  - Are you willing to do the boring along with the exciting?
  - How will you be when crisis strikes (and it will)?
  - How will you deal with being ill?
  - Is your social life predominantly work-related?

Continued

- How are you as an employer?
  - Are you willing to be the sole boss?
  - Will you take responsibility for others' welfare?
  - Are you able to delegate?
  - Can you provide motivation and discipline?
  - Are you able to provide a counselling service?
- How are you as an architect?
  - Do you need others to discuss (bounce around) ideas with?
  - Will you be able to stay up to date with professional, legal, etc. issues?
  - Are you happy promoting yourself/your firm?
  - Do you have a network of co-professionals to call upon?

For the partnership/company

- How are you together?
  - Do you get along as friends as well as professionals?
  - Have you worked closely together before?
  - Do you have complementary skills/personalities?
  - Is there an understanding as to who will do what task?
  - Are you able to recognise, acknowledge and accept each other's strengths and weaknesses?
  - What are the expectations on working hours, holidays, etc?
  - Will there be friction if one partner/director brings in or does more work than another?
  - Will there be friction if one partner/director gets more media attention than the other?
- How are you as employers?
  - As for the one-person practice (above)
- How are you as architects?
  - Do you see eye-to-eye on architectural style and quality?
  - Will you work together or separately?
  - Do you work well together?
  - And as for the one-person practice (above)

Feasibility tests – environmental and quality of life issues

Working at home

- Have you the space?
- What impression will it put across?
- Will you be able to concentrate in a domestic environment?
- Do you need a break/orientation time between home and work?
- Will you be able to 'leave work' at evenings/weekends?
- Will it provide you/your family with privacy?
- Will it be appropriate for visitors and staff (consider insurance and health and safety)?
- Will it restrict the practice's growth?

Renting premises

- What kind of location do you need?
- How close is it to your potential clients or to home?
- How and for how long will you or your staff travel?
- What facilities do you need (workspaces, reception, meeting room, library, kitchen, outside space, etc.)?
- For how long can you commit?
- What standard of space/facilities would you accept?
- Do you need room for enlargement/shrinkage?
- Are shared facilities an option?
- Do you want to be in a local community of other architects, etc?
- Do you need nearby cafés, pubs, print shops, etc?
- Do you need car parking/bike storage, etc?

Sustainability

- How much is the environment an issue to the practice?
- Does the practice need to show its environmental credentials in the way it operates?

Work–life balance

- Do you know how to switch off from work when necessary?
- Will you be able to take time off for holidays? (allow 4–6 weeks/year)
- What will happen if you are ill for a lengthy period?
- Can you arrange appropriate cover while you are away?

sectors, then you are likely to be better off working for a larger player. To work on such projects as a new practice, you will either need to have the specialist skills that bring your new firm into the teams implementing these projects or have great tenacity and persuasive powers. If your experience is with larger and the more complex building types and you want your new firm to continue to work on similar projects, then you will need to ensure that your business plan takes this aspiration fully into account.

See: Work Stage D: The business plan, page 23

Finally, some people are better suited to working for themselves than others. They apparently thrive on the risks and uncertainties that accompany starting up from scratch and can handle the potential loneliness of being outside an established business framework and office. Despite the importance of having specialist skills on which to market your new practice, running a firm also requires a high degree of multitasking and constant switching from one activity to another. Extended periods of time for concentrating on a single project or problem may become a luxury. As you become an employer you may need to recognise that your time will also belong to and be called upon by everyone else in the office, and that to have time to yourself you may need to deliberately carve out time to be alone, whether at home, in the office or elsewhere.

Before you make a career decision to start up for yourself, ensure that the many different pressures that running a business entails are for you.

Escape routes

Like getting married, starting a practice is relatively easy to do but is far more difficult to undo. Projects do not finish neatly together and tend to overlap with new ones, and issues such as maintaining run-off indemnity insurance tend to make continuing in practice always the most straightforward option. It can also be difficult to get back into paid employment at an appropriate level after you have been out of it for a while. There are exit routes, but the best ones rely on you having built up the business to a point of success where you can either hand it over to your partners or other staff or find an outside buyer. This is not always an option for the small practice, particularly near the beginning of the practice's life.

CHECKLIST

Work Stage A: Appraisal and feasibility

☐ Take a reality check and ask yourself and your partners the basic questions about why you want to start a practice, what you want to do, with whom and by when.

☐ Carry out a feasibility study looking at the various aspects of running a business: financial/economic, social and environmental. Examine the potential change to your quality of life.

☐ Make sure that running a business is for you and that you are prepared to do it for the long term.

Work Stage B
Preparing the brief

A short but essential section on getting the basics right before setting up your business – by preparing a written brief.

This guide encourages you to look at starting a new practice as a project to both design and implement. It is a project in which you will be client, designer, contractor and user – it will be worthwhile getting it right! All projects should start with a well-written brief, explaining what you seek to achieve from the venture, and setting up in business is no exception. Take off your architect's hat for the time being and concentrate on your aims and aspirations as the purchaser and user of a new business vehicle. The brief should go on to inform the business plan (Work Stage D) and ultimately determine the way you will run your business and carry out projects.

Brief essentials

The mission

- A short (five or six lines) statement of intent – ideally inspirational.

Objectives

- The means of achieving the mission – see Work Stage D for further discussion of objectives.

Performance requirements and measures

- Benchmarks and targets by which to assess and measure your achievements against your objectives.

Priorities

- Establishing what is important to you and the business. These could reflect principles, beliefs or core themes: e.g. sustainability, innovation, social commitment, treatment of staff, digital technology, etc.

Management of decisions and responsibilities

- Who is going to be responsible and for what?

Timeframe

- A programme for progress and development.

Who?

- Who should be involved?: including staff, colleagues, advisers, clients, etc.

Where?

- Both the office location(s) and the target area for your business.

CHECKLIST

Work Stage B: Preparing the brief

☐ Prepare a brief; write down in structured form a clear set of goals.

Work Stage C
The outline business case

This work stage deals with the preparatory work needed prior to developing a detailed business proposition, including SWOT analysis, advice, research and training. A business plan should start to develop, including the second iteration of the financial model.

Having decided to start up a new business, you need make the first stab at fleshing out your proposals. This is not a detailed exercise, it is roughly equivalent to preparing a sketch scheme. It investigates and establishes the basics, and may still leave you with a number of alternative options to pursue.

SWOT analysis

The SWOT (strengths, weaknesses, opportunities, threats) analysis is a well-tried and understood means of assessing where you stand and where you might go. It can be done by an individual working alone, but is also ideal to develop as a group, either in a structured discussion or brainstorming session. Involve anyone whom you believe might be able to contribute or will be affected. Tackle each section on its own and do not let either pessimism or optimism get the better of you. SWOT exercises should be repeated on a regular (at least yearly) basis as an evaluation tool as the firm is established and develops. An example of an SWOT analysis is given on the following pages.

Research

Carrying out your SWOT analysis will have required you to start researching the potential market for your services. This research will continue throughout the life of the practice, but at this stage it should still be relatively straightforward to get the type of information you will need before you are in a position to find and convince real clients to hire you.

Example SWOT analysis

Background

A number of locally experienced architects are joining forces to set up a new partnership. There is the prospect of reasonable work from a previous client and they have been offered workspace on a business park.

Evaluation

Strengths:

- Strong skills base developed from years of working on major projects for other firms
- Good contacts in the development sector
- Complementary mix of skills between proposed partners
- Expertise in cladding systems and education design
- Good local knowledge
- Hard-working ethic
- Business nous
- Offer of office space

Weaknesses:

- No previous experience running a business and little knowledge of business procedures
- Only large-project experience
- Proposed partners all of a similar age and background
- Lack of expertise in housing sector – the most likely source of work
- Low capital base (need to get healthy workflow)
- Imbalance between partners and staff (currently no staff)
- Office space in out-of-way location

Opportunities:

- Major house building programme locally – growth area
- Good relationship with local newspaper might lead to regular publicity or even a column
- Contact with previous client suggesting potential £500k project
- New local breakfast networking club proposed – opportunity to join at start
- Local ideas competition for town centre improvements
- Campaign for new arts centre – could offer pro bono design assistance
- Friendship/working relationship with firm of engineers might lead to joint projects
- Offer of ongoing project work from previous employers
- Part-time teaching job available
- Semi-retired local practitioner willing to act as practice mentor

Threats:

- Three long-established local firms dominate most of the available work in the vicinity (includes previous/current employers)
- Major projects in the area tend to be included in county-wide framework deals
- Only enough funds to survive for nine months without fees to cover overheads
- Local planning authority relatively hostile to innovative/modern proposals
- One proposed partner being wooed to stay at current practice to work on major arts project
- Most likely potential client is in financially precarious position

Continued

Assessment

There are adequate saleable skills among proposed partners, but the local area appears problematic, both in applicability of skills to local needs and the degree of market share in the hands of potential competitors. The partnership may need to look outside the local area to find projects that are a better match for partners' current skills. Current skill areas need to be kept engaged if they are to remain an asset (the location is an area of growth and so will require new schools in time).

Local clients may be persuaded over time, but they should not be relied on for immediate income. Marketing initiatives are potentially worthwhile, but the amount of time and resources they absorb must be carefully controlled. Alternative sources of income at early stages may be key to long-term survival. Thorough investigation of local opportunities may be useful – the mentor could be very useful for this. It will be important to develop new areas of skills to better match the future needs of the locality.

Actions

- Look for job opportunities within current areas of expertise, but be prepared to work further afield.
- Run credit check on potential client(s).
- Consider role as consultant to other design firms (e.g. on cladding).
- Develop marketing strategy, including competitions, etc.
- Network and make contacts.
- Explore opportunities for getting into local supply chains and framework deals.
- Improve understanding of long-term potential of local area (consider taking on mentor on a consultant basis).
- Consider alternative part-time employment (teaching, etc.) while practice finds its feet. One partner might stay in full-time employment for initial period.

Your main interest will be in the size of the market and the range of services that are likely to be in demand. Other professionals should be able to help you with this, both your own advisers and others; including solicitors, estate agents and local authority members and officers. Other construction professionals may also be happy to advise you on the market for architects' services. You may even find that some architects are prepared to offer advice, despite some of them being potential long-term competitors.

You will need to size up the strength and character of the competition you are likely to come up against. This will be relatively straightforward if you are proposing a rural or town practice based on the local area, with a definable number of firms, whether architects or others, in practice locally. It will be more difficult in a large city, with many existing practices and a host of specialties and peculiarities.

This is a time for wide ranging discussion and exploration, not only to evaluate your potential market, but also to discover how the type of businesses you may be dealing with work in practice: how they find their clients; the workstyles that work for them; relationships with clients; how fees are structured; and what the challenges are for a business in the location and the fields you envisage.

Advice

Get advice. This is worth saying again. Get advice. It comes in many forms, from legal and financial to branding and managerial. Some of it may be good, some well-meaning and some downright bad. You will need enough advice to be able to tell the difference and to make your own judgments, without being overwhelmed by different voices.

Some advice may be specific and come from those who may become an essential part of your business set-up (your bank manager, solicitor, accountant, etc.) and with whom you may choose to stay associated with for the long term. Other advice is more general and available from published sources, business presentations and courses, as well as from government-sponsored organisations such as Business Link. Business Link will also respond to requests for advice and send out expert mentors to advise on particular issues, such as finance, law, etc.

There is a welter of advice available; in books, in newspaper articles, on websites, from firms selling their services and from individuals hoping to promote themselves. The quality and applicability of advice will vary considerably.

Business training

From your preliminary analysis, of both your current skills and the market you are planning to enter, you may decide that it would be useful, or even essential, to get training before or soon after you start your business. Some practitioners have put themselves through rigorous management courses, or even obtained MBAs, prior to starting their firms; others have enrolled on shorter courses.

There is a wide range of courses available, including the RIBA's Business Master-classes and many others specific to the business of architecture, such as marketing or running an effective practice. General business skills training packages are also provided by many organisations, and grants may be available (see www.businesslink.gov.uk). If your education to date has been mainly architectural, then it is more than possible that you will not have had any business training to speak of, and this may be the time to take your first course. Do not be put off if it does not seem immediately applicable to the design profession; it will be useful, even if it only helps you to better understand your clients' thinking and motivations.

Investment and risk

Your initial budget analysis will have generated questions about your start-up costs, including equipment costs. You need to begin to plan your strategy for this. Are you going to start small and cheaply and build up gradually and organically, investing in bigger and better over time, or are you going to start with a big splash, investing heavily and showing real commitment from the outset – death or glory! – or will it be somewhere in between? The same will apply to your choice of premises. If you start from a room at home there is every chance you will get stuck there, but if you take on an office good enough to let a client see, the expense might be enough to sink your fledgling firm.

Work out, taking into account the advice you have obtained, how much you are prepared to risk to get your new business off the ground. What level of investment are you prepared to put in and how long can you go before you start to get break even and then pay it back? Are you willing to remortgage your house to provide investment, or even risk losing it altogether if the business fails? This is a sensitive area that needs to be discussed with all those potentially affected, including family as well as business partners, financial advisers, bank manager, etc. It will influence not only the size and scope of your plans, but also the business model you ultimately decide to use.

The outline business case (OBC)

By this stage you should be starting to see the shape of your proposed business, if only in outline. Commit it to paper, describing your aims and goals and how you envisage the character of the business: its ethos and style. Who will be its clients, and where in the market will it sit? What are the timescales and intentions for growth/stability? Where would you like your practice to be in five or ten years' time? Some of your plan will be general and aspirational, other parts more precise and thought out. Not too much detail is required in the plan at this stage, but it should include a further iteration of your cost plan, as you accept or reject options for the firm's future.

An OBC topic list

- Strategic objectives
- Proposed key personnel, skills and strengths, past successes
- Proposed advisers
- Services to be offered
- Market for services and barriers to entry
- The competition
- Opportunities
- Threats and risks
- Business strategy
- Proposed business structure and management skills
- Marketing approach
- Training plan
- Growth plan
- Staff recruitment and requirements
- Premises
- Financial plan and projections
- Investment required
- Sources of potential investment
- Long-term aims

These topics will be developed further in Work Stage D, the business plan.

┌─────────── **CHECKLIST** ───────────┐

Work Stage C: The outline business case

☐ Do a SWOT (strengths/weaknesses/opportunities/threats) analysis.
☐ Seek advice.
☐ Carry out market research – into both services required and the level of demand for them.
☐ Size up and understand the potential competition.
☐ Assess your own skills and knowledge and get appropriate training to fill any gaps.
☐ Establish a basic risk and investment strategy.
☐ Prepare an outline business case for your proposed firm, describing in general terms your approach to all aspects of the business.

Work Stage D
The business plan

This work stage concentrates on putting together the business plan in a format that will be comprehensible both to the practice and to potential funders, bankers, etc. Topics that should be covered by the business plan include: company history and arrangements, business objectives, advisers, business potential and competition, services to be offered, distinctiveness, pricing structure, capacity, promotion, size and growth, company structure and management, law and regulation, finances, funding and naming.

The business plan

Preparing a good business plan is an essential step. Do not start work without one.

- Preparing a business plan gives you the opportunity to lay out why you are starting up a business, what you are going to achieve, how you aim to do so, when goals will be achieved, and how much it is going to cost and then return in profit.
- You need to go through the business plan process to ensure that you have got your thinking straight.
- Having the business plan written down allows others to check that it makes sense and advise you further.
- The business plan will be the main tool for raising finance and investment for your business.
- It will become a benchmark to check your progress against over the years of practice and a useful reminder for when matters start to run adrift.
- Developed versions of the plan can be presented to bank managers, funders and the like to explain the status, intentions and financial requirements of your business.

Nonetheless many architects practise for years before developing any business plan at all. Many others never get round to it. This may explain why so many start-ups in architecture stay so relatively unprofitable. Yet there is nothing final or cast in stone about such a plan; even having a preliminary strategy in place for the first two or three years of practice, to be replaced by a more mature and considered plan once there is real experience to base it on, is strongly recommended.

Work out your business plan with care – see it as one of your most significant design challenges. Seek out good advice; you are unlikely to be an expert in

See: Advisers, page 26

setting up and managing a business – it is not your discipline after all. This is an opportunity to start and forge long-lasting relationships with advisers who can help you over the many years of business ahead.

Much of the thinking in your business plan should flow from the preliminary SWOT analysis you carried out during the early stages of deciding to set up a

See: SWOT analysis, page 15

new architectural business, but it should now be elaborated and transformed into a fully rounded proposition; it will, after all, shape your job and should become a dominant part of your life for the foreseeable future.

The business plan can be split into six sections, as follows:

- The company
  - existing arrangements, history, personnel, skills, premises, etc.
  - business objectives
  - advisers
- Business potential
  - market
  - research
  - clients
  - competitors
- Your offer
  - services to be provided
  - distinctiveness in the market
  - pricing structure
  - capacity
- Promotion and marketing
- Business arrangements
  - company structure
  - management
  - rules and regulations
  - size and growth
- Finance
  - money management
  - overheads
  - financial forecast
  - funding
  - fee collection

The company

Existing arrangements, history, personnel, skills, premises, etc.

In starting a new company you will not be setting out from scratch. You may already have established links with potential clients and other useful contacts. You will certainly have valuable skills and experience and you are likely to have a background that will prove useful in launching a new venture. You may even already have premises – even if it is simply space in your own home.

Lay all this out in written form, partly to establish where you are starting from, but also to remind you, your colleagues and advisers, what you have to base your business on and to build from. You may want to do something very different in your new business, but begin by knowing yourself better. This may also be helpful for learning more about your proposed partners, and will be especially important if several of you are coming together to set up a new firm. You may not know each other as well as you thought, and sharing background information may not only be helpful to the business but key to developing and maintaining good personal relationships.

Note: If your firm is already established, this becomes an even more essential element of your plan and you can, and should, include copious information on your performance and track record to date.

Business objectives

Carefully consider your business goals, and set them out either as a list or in diagrammatic form. You should already have begun to articulate these goals in your brief to yourself in Work Stage B. They may be high-level aspirations or very specific achievement targets, but they should be relatively few in number and expressed in a straightforward way. They will need to be agreed among all the principal players, but buy-in from employees (if you have any) will be important and you may also want to consult on, test and explain them more widely among clients, friends and family. Your business goals need to be forward-looking, robust and capable of standing the test of time.

Peter Barber of Peter Barber Architects defined his objectives (albeit several years after establishing his practice) as:

- to create delightful and beautiful architecture
- to maintain an adequate level of living
- to grow without threatening the quality of the work.

Alternatively you may have more specific aims, such as:

- winning a certain number or value of jobs per quarter
- achieving predetermined client satisfaction levels
- delivering minimum added value on identified projects
- winning at least one industry award per year
- achieving employee satisfaction targets
- growing to a significant size in the industry.

Some of the goals may be aspirational, others ruthlessly practical. They are needed so that your planning can be focused on achieving them, and later on you can assess whether they have been reached. All goals should have a time-scale. Some may be permanent features of a long-term plan and must be checked against on a regular basis, others will have a 'sell-by' date and so will eventually have to be replaced by new goals.

In general keep your general business goals separate from your financial ones.

See: Finances, page 46

Financial success may figure as an essential business aim, financial survival certainly should, but making money is a different level of concern to other business objectives and focusing on financial objectives may serve to obscure them.

Advisers

The importance of good advice and advisers has already been discussed, and in the eyes of potential investors or clients the credibility of your business proposition may depend on the backing of heavyweight advisers. Depending on the size and nature of your business, some advisers will be an absolute necessity, others a good idea and strongly to be recommended and still others a luxury but possibly worthwhile.

Your bank manager is likely to be one of your essential advisers and may well be needed as an ally in the years ahead. Banks have a wealth of experience of both successful and unsuccessful businesses and have a vested interest in ensuring that their customers are successful. Use their support to help your company grow and to avoid the numerous pitfalls in your way. But first you need to

See also: Bank account, page 69

choose your bank. Use the time prior to starting up to interview different banks to see what they can offer you, how sympathetic they are likely to be to design businesses and whether they will have appropriate staff available to be of useful assistance when needed.

Useful advisers

Other useful advisers may include the following:

- Solicitor – for legal, contractual and business advice, including company set-up arrangements and liability protection.
- Business adviser – to help you with all those business issues that never got mentioned on an architecture course, including, for example, marketing, negotiations, profitability, investment and risk.
- Accountant – you may do much of the work on this yourself but you should still have someone to help you through the detail and regulations of company accounts, VAT, etc. and to establish the best trading and tax arrangements for the business.
- Insurance broker – may be essential to both save you money and help you avoid and get out of trouble.
- PR consultant – to help you establish and then promote the right image and information about your firm.
- Professional organisations, such as the RIBA and ACA – publish standards and codes, guidance, business information, etc., and also organise conferences, seminars and training events. They will also deal with specific queries via their information lines or free telephone access to specialist advisers, and they may even take up your problems on behalf of the whole profession.
- Government sponsored organisations, such as:
  - Business Link
  - the Small Business Service
  - Constructing Excellence.
  These organisations publish extensive guidance on many aspects of starting and running businesses. Business Link will also provide experts to advise on specific issues.
- Co-professionals – may provide friendly useful advice as and when required, or may possibly take on a practice mentoring role to help nurture a new business.
- Local trade groups, such as chambers of commerce – may provide local information and also job leads.

Many, if not most, architectural practices go through patches when the fees are not coming in as expected, maybe because projects have become delayed or because clients have their own problems with cash flow. At these times having your bank manager on your side may well decide your financial survival. Your manager or bank business adviser needs to understand the way your business works and to realise that you know what you are doing. Be prepared to keep them, as individuals, regularly updated on your situation and your projected cash flow, especially when you can see rocky times ahead.

But recognise that banks are businesses as well, and are not by nature altruistic. They can pull the plug on you or make life difficult if they suspect that you are not a good prospect. It is also their role to make money by selling you a variety of services. Some of these you will actively want, but others may be superfluous or can be obtained at better rates elsewhere. It is in your interest to build a good working relationship with your bank and its staff, but know the limitations of the relationship and be prepared to start again elsewhere if necessary.

Business potential

The market

What and where is the market for your services? How large and how widespread might it be? You may already have a feel for this if you have been working for a company practising in the same area or have lived in the locality of your proposed new firm. But you need to dig deeper and do your homework on where your work will come from. This will include the geographical area you want to work in, the types of projects and range of clients. If you are proposing to sell a specialist service you may have to be able to travel to access a wider market than if you are planning a broad-based local service. You also need to check on your competition and the potential for collaboration with others.

Architecture is inevitably a business about place and people. It cannot all be done at the end of a phone or via computer networks. You have to meet your clients, visit building sites and discuss matters directly with local planners and builders. In any area there will be a level of current and likely future building activity. Will it be enough to keep you, and any likely competitors, busy? How large might that area be? Alternatively, how far, or for how long, are you willing to travel to carry out work? This may in turn depend on the size of the project and the fees and expenses it will carry.

Look at where you can easily travel to from your chosen base. Draw one hour, two hour and greater travel areas on maps. These are unlikely to be simple circles as good roads, or even local airports, may radically extend your reach in certain directions. Alternatively, turn this around to work out where to locate your firm in relation to good market locations.

Research

In assessing the potential for selling your services in the marketplace you should be prepared to spend time and effort doing research. If well directed, it is unlikely to be wasted.

Speak to any existing or potential clients. Speak to those who commission design and who require buildings. Find out how they chose their architects or procure their buildings and how they plan to do so in future. What are they looking for when they make their selection? Talk to other architects in the area, and also to engineers, surveyors and other construction consultants, planners and estate agents, etc. The regional office of the RIBA may well be a useful source of information, or consider attending RIBA regional or branch events and meetings. Identify from magazines and the local press the types of clients that are appointing the type of architects who you would consider your peers and likely competitors. Try to develop as full a picture of the building design and construction activity in your chosen area as possible. Who are the key firms and individuals? Where are decisions made? What are the lines of communication?

All of this is much easier to do before you set up your business; before you develop business relationships or are in competition with your potential informants. It is also easier to ask the innocent question when you are new and are not already selling a service. Do not waste the opportunity.

Try to discover whether any likely building programmes are coming up. Are the local authorities considering capital spending programmes? Will there be business investment in the area? How is the local housing market? Are any areas due for regeneration? Find out the likely procurement routes – if design and build looks like an option then this may be the time to meet potential bidding contractors. Make sure you get a good working knowledge of the economy and how it relates to potential design work.

Become familiar with the press and media and with other sources of local information, such as local authority websites. Find out where decision-makers get their information and advice. Make contact with journalists and opinion formers. Attend local events and meetings, join groups and organisations as far as is reasonable. Get your ear to the ground and gather information.

Clients

Clients come in many guises; from private individuals extending their houses and with little experience of architects, to large organisations with books of rules and guidelines as to what, where and how their consultants should do what they do. Equally, there are very organised small clients and there are large bodies with no idea of how to commission or work with architects. A recent and significant arrival among potential major clients is the contractor that carries out design and build work or acts as a single point contact for commissioning clients. In formulating your business plan you need to decide who are the right clients for your company.

You should aim to establish a broad client base. Few architects would survive for long on work from only one client, however good, or even from a single client sector – there would be too many peaks and troughs in demand to maintain a reasonably regular workflow. An ideal mix contains both private and public sector clients and, that highly desirable commodity, the regular provider of background bread-and-butter commissions. A diversity of clients, and therefore jobs, is also useful in order to avoid pigeonholing, which can threaten the development of a practice's reputation.

As you research potential clients also investigate their advisers. Who is preparing shortlists for them to select from? Do the local authorities maintain preselected lists of consultants or do they operate framework agreements? How do they maintain these lists – can anyone apply or is there a selection and qualification procedure?

For your initial business plan you will need to decide on the sectors you plan to pitch for work in, and ensure that there is a match between your skills and experience and the requirements and needs of your likely client base. The public sector has become more difficult to get work from as new public procurement regimes have taken hold, but there are nonetheless plenty of opportunities if you persevere. Some public sector organisations have a regular need for architects to work on small (and sometimes very small) projects.

Consider that almost all your existing clients can become repeat clients in time. They may eventually be a vital source of both work and referrals, and should be the best advertisement for your practice. Treat them with respect from the outset. Factor looking after them into your business plan, and do not neglect them, even when there are other, more alluring, clients in prospect.

The competition

Uncovering the potential competition will probably be a great deal easier than working out who the potential clients are. Remember, however, that competitors may also become collaborators or advisers on some projects, or even friends with whom you can commiserate when things have gone disastrously wrong. Competitors may have a range of approaches and come from different professional backgrounds. You may be as much in competition with a local builder as with another firm of architects. Examine each competitor's place in the market for design and other services and establish how your position can be differentiated from theirs.

Your offer

The services you plan to provide

Should you be about to start a small manufacturing or service business the most important issue would be the product or service you intended to sell. The same is true for setting up an architectural firm. There is a core service that you are likely to offer, but you may not want to do the very smallest of jobs and you are unlikely to be offered the largest. Similarly you may prefer to concentrate on just part of the standard service – many architects choose to go as far as obtaining planning consent for projects but no further – or you may have other services or specialisms you wish to sell. There is no standard model, or at least there should not be.

You need to do:

- what you do best
- what you can offer economically or at profit to the practice
- what you feel confident you can sell
- what there is, or will be, a market for.

This part of the business plan will take some work, including gathering intelligence on your likely market, but you will be in a far better position when you have developed it. You may even be introduced to future clients in the course of your investigations.

Start with what you know you can do and what you want to continue with. Add potential services that you feel confident you can develop or know how to obtain. Finally, list those services you would like to provide in the future but have yet to develop the capacity or experience to offer. The same exercise can be done for sectors and specialisms. It may be useful to start from a basic document, such as the *RIBA Plan of Work*, but list enthusiasms, skills and abilities that are outside standard frameworks as they may suggest directions for your practice that are particular to you and may make your practice stand out from the crowd.

It will also be important to assess the opportunities for selling your services, and to find those elusive gaps in the market. Discover which sectors are in growth or decline, and be clear on procurement routes and selection criteria and whether your firm can become a provider to clients using them. The considerations for a public sector-led programme are very different from private sector or developer markets. You may need to develop your services accordingly.

As a result of the liberalisation of professional barriers that has occurred over recent decades and the widening of market opportunities an architect can choose to provide many more services than are shown on the conventional schedule of architectural services or are listed in the curriculum of an architecture course. Technology, in turn, has greatly assisted this. Consider the full range of options available to you, from the material to the virtual and the physical to the cerebral. Put together a plan that contains not only what you really want to produce, but also what your customers will really want to buy from you; a match between the services you can or want to offer, the demand and the competition.

Distinctiveness

Having started to develop your offer of services you may hope and expect that clients will beat a path to your door to buy them. But they may find it disappointingly difficult to differentiate you from your competitors, who are offering a similar package of activities and potentially a lower price. You will need to ensure that your offer has an added edge and that you mark yourself out as being distinctive and identifiably different. Clients and customers need a good reason to come to you rather than go to one of the many other architectural firms they could have chosen.

Marketeers have developed an entire language to describe this area, including advanced concepts of 'brand', 'reputation' and 'unique selling points' (USPs). Issues of branding and reputation are discussed in Work Stage G, but as you develop your potential schedule of services, consider what you have to offer that would make you emerge from the pack of your competitors. What do you have to offer that is an advance on the norm or that might be otherwise difficult to find in your business area?

*See:
Marketing,
page 87*

Possible USPs might include a specialism that you can already offer or are prepared to develop, a particular understanding or interest that you can bring to your work or the integration of your architectural skills with another area, such as development or manufacture. Note that architects tend to have a far stronger belief than their customers in the value of design quality and style to mark them out from the herd. You cannot rely on this alone, especially in the early days, before you have developed your *carefully nurtured* reputation.

Approach this from a client's point of view. They will be looking for an excellent service that offers them a business advantage or a better home; they are very unlikely to be considering appointing you to further your career or to give you the opportunity to exercise your creative talent. Your selling points have to be ones that appeal to your clients first and foremost. It is a bonus if they also appeal to you and your peers.

Pricing structure

As part of your business plan you will need to consider how much you intend to sell your services for. Pricing tends to be largely dependent on what the market will bear, but you also need to be aware of how much the production and delivery of a service is costing you: in time, resources and overheads. There is often very little relationship between the value of a service to a client and the expense to you as supplier. You therefore need to have a position on how to quote and to charge for your work.

There are three traditional approaches to calculating fees: as a percentage of construction costs, on a time basis (at an agreed rate per hour) or as a lump sum quoted for a service, and it is common for fees to be expressed as a combination of two or all three of these approaches. All of these methods are problematic as they neither reflect the value of the service, nor (with the exception of the time charge) the cost of providing it. Certainly they do not help you to cost or value your service. You may want to consider fresh ways of valuing and charging for what you do.

Research the market; find out how others charge for their work and how the work is valued by their paying customers. Discuss alternative methods of charging with clients and potential clients and discover where they see the greatest value delivered from the architectural service.

The RIBA publishes its annual research on fees charged for architects' services across a range of sectors. This is available in detail, at a cost, from the researchers Mirza & Nacey, but greatly abbreviated figures are also published in the *RIBA Journal*. Charge-out rates for staff at different levels of seniority are published in a number of journals.

Transparency in charging is important, especially should there be any dispute about it at a later date. Several firms charge on the basis of a pre-published schedule of charges. For example, the franchise network Architectyourhome has a menu of services on its website that potential clients are invited to select from at predetermined cost. Alternatively, some firms have successfully charged on the basis of value delivered to their clients or shared with them in the risk of a development.

Take care not to undersell yourself – if you develop a reputation for giving design ideas away cheaply, or even for free, it can be difficult to charge effectively for providing more of the same. Unfortunately, the UK is full of badly paid architecture practices which are not charging adequate fees or valuing their services highly enough – do not let your practice join them.

Most clients will have very little idea of what an architect does all day to justify apparently enormous fees. When it comes to negotiating your fee agreement with your client, consider explaining in detail the tasks you will undertake on their behalf. It may come as a shock to you too when you consider how long it takes to fill in standard documents or write contractual correspondence. It may also be worthwhile offering some clients the opportunity to do part of the work themselves – they are likely to value your contribution all the more.

Capacity

As part of your offer you will need to consider the resource and capacity level you intend to make available and, most importantly, the perception of that capacity by a potential client. There has been a recent trend for clients not to use small companies for many of their projects, possibly because they overestimate the staff numbers required for a project (and architects do not generally seek to disabuse clients of the sense of importance that a project has in their minds) and also because they want a resource 'safety net' in case of accident, illness, etc.

There is clearly some correlation between the size of a practice and its ability to deal with its workload – whether a multiplicity of small jobs or a single project that has to be completed within weeks rather than months or years – but it tends to be exaggerated. A well-motivated small team can achieve prodigious amounts of work if needs be. Plan to be large enough so that you can attract the jobs you want and know how to handle them when they do come in. Obtaining the capacity to cope can generally be dealt with, if necessary through a mixture of hiring, growth and contracting out workload – the most difficult part is getting the job in the first place.

Being and staying the right size is one of the more intractable problems of running an architectural practice – the expression 'feast or famine' comes up a lot in discussion between practitioners. Beware of expanding to deal with a peak in workflow only to shrink rapidly afterwards; it can be very damaging to office morale. Similarly, periods of underemployment of staff, such as while waiting for that vital project go-ahead, are not only bad for the cash flow but can also lead to contagious disaffection. If you do plan for growth, steady expansion and a sustained workload to match should be built into your plan, but you should also assume a high degree of volatility in your workflow.

Practice promotion

In drawing up your business plan you will need to consider how you will promote the firm. No work will come in if no one has ever heard of you. Prepare a strategy for selling (however softly) your business. Your plan should include the production of promotional material, achieving standard measurable 'wins', such as getting positive press coverage, winning awards and networking, as well as other and more creative ways of establishing your name. Your promotional style should be your own, but make sure it is effective.

Include an amount in your financial plan for promotional activities, expressed either as an annual sum, a sum per employee or a percentage of turnover. Inevitably almost any amount will be small compared with the task of establishing your profile, so you will have to make it work hard. But having a definite sum will encourage a focused marketing strategy, and having a cap will help to make sure it is spent effectively.

Allow for getting feedback on your promotional effort. This might be a record of press coverage, a log of enquiries coming in from individual promotions (advertisements in the Yellow Pages, your website, involvement in exhibitions, etc.) and their conversion rate into paying work, or client feedback on the service being given or offered.

See: Work Stage G: Getting noticed, page 87 — Marketing is discussed at much greater length in the section on getting work. The reason for including it here is to stress its important role in the overall business plan. Without a marketing and promotional strategy your business is without a thought-through approach to reaching its customers and so may not survive long.

Business arrangements

Size and growth

What size of company do you want to be and by when? The right size may be suggested by the kind of work you want to win, but this is not necessarily conclusive. The number of founding partners or directors might equally suggest a size, once you have established a reasonable partner to staff ratio. Equally, group dynamics may suggest an ideal working size. Management gurus wax lyrical about the perfect size for an effective team. This is not to suggest you

See: Capacity, page 34

can accurately control the size of the company, which will fluctuate with workload and other influencing factors, but you need to plan for the future and it will be an important feature of how your business runs.

A two- or three-person company needs a very different approach from a six- to ten-person firm or bigger concern. Some of the issues of growth can be dealt with over time, but it is very difficult to retrofit office management routines once you are underway – projects still have to be delivered while a new management system is being introduced. If you are planning to grow relatively quickly then run your firm that way from the start, ensure you have office space to grow into and that your systems can adapt as you do so. This may mean higher overheads and more elaborate procedures than necessary during the growth period, but it will be worth it.

Alternatively, if you are planning to stay small from the start then choose simpler systems and keep your overheads down. You are less likely to need complex filing procedures, elaborate accounting programs or lengthy human resources and quality assurance policies. You may need versions of all the things that larger practices have but they can be kept much more straightforward and relatively inexpensive, despite what the sales people tell you.

Company structure

You are setting up a business. You will need to decide how to operate legally. What business vehicle are you going to travel in? You have four main options (although there are some other choices, such as becoming a charity or operating from overseas, which are not discussed further). The four options – all of which have pros and cons, and some will be better than others for the various approaches to and sizes of business – are as follows:

- Sole trader – the most simple and straightforward arrangement with a minimum of form filling. You are in charge and directly responsible for everything, which means that all your possessions and home are at risk if you cannot pay your debts. You can also be made bankrupt. Despite the title, a sole trader can take on employees. Your most likely tax status will be as self-employed, although this will need to be confirmed.

- Partnership – a fairly traditional arrangement for an architects' firm with two or more people setting up a business together. Partners share personal responsibility, but like the sole trader they also carry all the risk. In a partnership this comes with the added onus of joint and several liability, meaning that any one partner can be liable for all the debts of the partnership should the other partners not be able to pay their share. As one partner can make business decisions on behalf of all the other partners they can also leave them, unknowingly, with all the risk and responsibility. Liability remains after a partnership is dissolved or when partners retire, or even die (when it will fall upon the partners' estates).

Under the Partnership Act 1890 there is no legal requirement for a written partnership agreement, however it is usual for a formal agreement or 'deed of partnership' to be drawn up, setting out rights and responsibilities. The deed would normally be prepared by a solicitor, but the bones of it should be agreed in advance by the proposed partners. The deed should deal with issues such as:

- the individual responsibilities of partners
- apportioning of profits and losses
- repayment and interest on capital invested
- retirement of and pension arrangements for partners
- the admission of new partners.

Even such issues as the number of days of holiday per year to be taken should be considered. Ensure the deed includes clauses to deal with dispute resolution, just in case arguments develop and processes such as arbitration be required. Take professional advice on the contents and preparation of a partnership agreement/deed.

- Limited liability partnership (LLP) – a new form of partnership bought in by the Limited Liability Partnerships Act of 2000. It is part way between a partnership and a limited liability company and combines aspects of both. The key aspect that has made it a relatively popular trading structure for architects is that it restricts the liability of the partners to the combined amount that each has invested or personally guaranteed to raise. Management and tax responsibilities are much the same as for partnerships and, similarly, a deed of partnership is strongly recommended.

An LLP is regarded as a separate legal entity from the individual partners and will externally be treated as such. It is necessary to register it with the Registrar of Companies by filling out a standard form and payment of a small fee. Annual accounts must to be sent to the Registrar and they will be available for public inspection. Auditing of the accounts is formally required, but most small companies are likely to be exempt from this. No directors are required, but at least two designated partners (or 'members' in the language of the Limited Liability Partnerships Act) will be required to act in roles similar to those of company secretary and director.

- Limited Liability Company (Ltd) – a legal entity owned by its shareholders and which protects the individual members/shareholders from personal responsibility for the debts of the company beyond the notional value of the shareholding and any personal guarantees. A company has a formal structure, with a board of directors (at least one) and a company secretary. Although generally protected from the debts and obligations of the company, directors are required to show a duty of care to the company, and if they fail in this they may be found liable for debts or be disqualified from acting as a company director in other companies.

The company structure allows for the raising of capital for the firm by the selling of shares in the company to external investors. It also allows non-shareholders to be appointed as directors, allowing younger (and poorer) employees of practices to be appointed to senior positions. The management structure of the company allows for directors and similar appointees to be changed relatively easily, without having to dissolve and reform or for new agreements to be drawn up. Companies must submit annual accounts and tax returns to HM Revenue and Customs and will be required to pay the resultant corporation tax. Annual accounts and further details on the company must also be sent to Companies House. Before setting up a company take legal and financial advice. A memorandum of association and articles of association need to be prepared to cover a number of essential issues, and standard registration documents must be submitted along with the standard fees.

Few architects starting up in practice would currently consider immediately forming a limited company as a trading structure. Yet it does have some significant advantages, even if it requires complying with a formal pre-set business structure and does not have the immediate management flexibility and lack of bureaucracy of a partnership. Most business start-ups in the UK have no hesitation in adopting the limited company structure and as professional consultancies slowly become like other businesses this form of trading is set to become a more likely choice.

Note: Company directors and secretaries have wide legal responsibilities. See guidance prepared by Companies House, in particular guidance booklet GBA1, for more details: www.companieshouse.gov.uk.

Any decision as to which business structure to form needs careful consideration. Take advice and research the advantages and disadvantages of the alternatives. There is no bar to changing company structure at a later date, but this can be awkward and may affect client confidence. Start with a company structure that you think will last you at least for the first five to ten years of practice.

Comparison of business structures

	Sole trader	Partnership	Limited liability partnership (LLP)	Limited liability company (private company limited by shares)
Registration	None required	None required	Incorporation required at Companies House	Incorporation required at Companies House
Registration information required	None	None	Name of LLP Address of the registered office of the LLP Name, full address and date of birth of each member Names of the formally appointed 'designated' members (minimum two)	A memorandum of association (including the company's name, objects and location of the registered office) Articles of association (the rules for governing the company's affairs) Address of the registered office Names of director(s) and the company secretary, including full addresses, dates of birth, occupations and details of other directorships held within the past five years (Form 10) A statutory declaration of compliance with legal requirements (Form 12)
Relevant legislation	None	Partnership Act 1890	Limited Liability Partnerships Act 2000 and Limited Liability Partnerships Regulations 2001	Companies Acts 1985 and 1989 and subsequent amendments
Legal status	No status	No status	A separate legal entity	A separate legal entity
Ownership	By sole trader	Equally between partners, unless otherwise agreed in deed of partnership	Equally between members, unless otherwise agreed in deed of partnership	By members (shareholders)
Legal agreements	None	Deed of partnership: not required but strongly recommended	Deed of partnership: not required but very strongly recommended	Memorandum of association and articles of association

Administrative requirements	Keeping records of income and outgoings Registration with HM Revenue and Customs as self-employed	Keeping records of income and outgoings Registration with HM Revenue and Customs as self-employed	Annual accounts and a return giving key details on the LLP and its members, to be made to Companies House	Annual accounts and a return giving key details on the company and its directors, to be made to Companies House Companies House must be informed of certain other changes including: new shares allotted, special or extraordinary resolutions passed and mortgages entered into
Management structure	Minimal	Minimal	No limit to number of 'members' of partnership, but at least two must be 'designated members'	A director or board of directors, who have certain legal responsibilities A minimum of one director and a company secretary to be appointed officers of the company
Liability	Full responsibility for business debts with unlimited liability Homes and possessions are at risk	Personal responsibility for business debts with unlimited liability Partners have joint and several liability making all partners fully and individually responsible for debts Partners' homes and possessions are at risk	Liability for business debts is limited to the total of monies invested in and guaranteed to the business Individual liability can remain in tort	Liability for business debts is limited to the total of monies invested in and guaranteed to the business Directors can be held responsible if they have not carried out their proper duties and might be disqualified from holding directorships in other companies Individual liability can remain in tort
Privacy	No public disclosure requirement	No public disclosure requirement	Company accounts and other information, including on remuneration, provided to Companies House is publicly available	Company accounts and other information, including on remuneration, provided to Companies House is publicly available

Continued

Comparison of business structures (continued)

	Sole trader	Partnership	Limited liability partnership (LLP)	Limited liability company (private company limited by shares)
Change at the top	No bureaucracy, but change will effectively mean a new start	If one of the partners changes (or resigns, dies or goes bankrupt) then the partnership will be dissolved. The business can continue when a new partnership is formed	Companies House must be informed (on the appropriate form) if: • a new member, or designated member, is appointed or changed • there are any changes in members' names, addresses or other details Any deed of partnership may also require amendment	Companies House must be informed (on the appropriate form) if: • a new officer is appointed • an officer resigns from the company • there are changes in an officer's name or address or other details
Profits	Belong to the sole trader	To be shared equally by the partners unless otherwise specified	To be shared equally by the members unless otherwise specified	To be shared by the members (shareholders) as specified
Tax (generally)	Self-employed tax and National Insurance (NI) status for sole trader PAYE for any employees	Self-employed tax and NI status for partners PAYE for employees	Self-employed tax and NI status for partners PAYE for employees	Corporation tax PAYE for directors and employees
Employees	Normal procedure – it is not a problem for a sole trader to have employees	Normal procedure	Normal procedure	Directors treated as employees of company
Duties	None	None	Accounts must be audited annually (but exemption is possible)	Accounts must be audited annually (but exemption is possible) Registers of members, directors, directors' interests and charges, etc. to be kept

Naming	Free to choose within legal limits: • should not be the same as, or very similar to, another local business • must contain no offensive or sensitive words • must not include the words 'limited' or 'plc' or any equivalents	Free to choose within legal limits: • should not be the same as, or very similar to, another local business • must contain no offensive or sensitive words • must not include the words 'limited' or 'plc' or any equivalents	LLP name must be registered: • must include the word 'limited liability partnership' or 'LLP' (or equivalent) at the end of the name • must not be the same as, or very similar to, another name in the company or LLP names index • must contain no offensive words • certain sensitive words require consent before use	Company name must be registered: • must include the word 'limited' or 'Ltd' (or equivalent) at the end of the name • must not be the same as, or very similar to, another name in the company or LLP names index • must contain no offensive words • certain sensitive words require consent before use
Stationery (including letterheads, e-mails, bills, invoices, etc. – see appropriate guidance)	Name and business address If not trading under own name, must include own name on business stationery	Name and business address If not trading under own names, must include partners' names on business stationery	Must show legibly: • business name • place of registration and registration number • the fact that the business is a limited liability partnership • the address of the registered office	Must show legibly: • business name • place of registration and registration number Note: the company does not have to state the directors' names on stationery, but if it does it is required to state them all
Name plates	Your name should be clearly displayed	Your name should be clearly displayed	All places of business are required to conspicuously and legibly display the LLP's name on the outside	All places of business are required to conspicuously and legibly display the company's names on the outside

Note: This is only a guide. You must get legal and tax advice as appropriate and contact Companies House (www.companieshouse.gov.uk) for further advice.

Management

Along with a business structure and general legal and tax regulations come a variety of management requirements. A business has to keep accounts, a company needs to appoint directors, health and safety regulations must be adhered to, insurance has to be maintained and so on. But the real management requirement is to run the practice in such a way that:

- it achieves its aims
- skills and resources are well organised
- it has the capacity to develop and grow.

Whatever the size of the practice, both the overall business and any individual projects need some degree of planning and allocation of resources. This will be as critical for a one-person practice, where time is in particularly short supply, as for a multi-person firm where different activities can be the responsibilities of defined groups or individuals. If the practice has, or will have, staff they will need to be led and inspired and their ambitions recognised and accommodated.

Do not underestimate the amount of time that business management can take. It is time spent on tasks that are not essentially productive, but which are necessary in order for the practice to be so. It is an activity that is not traditionally popular with architects: their training rarely equips them for the role and it can keep them away from designing. If you are starting a new business and have not had experience of taking the responsibility for either running projects or a business unit or managing staff or teams, then discuss this with those who have. Build up a picture of what may be required, whether it is preparing VAT accounts or filing documents, or interviewing, managing and even firing staff.

Individual management issues are dealt with in Work Stage E.

Rules and regulations

Starting a new business means signing up to a wide range of rules and regulations, although it is likely that you will previously have had no more than a general awareness of many of them. As well as the legal requirements, you may also have to comply with the requirements of insurers, clients and landlords and the codes issued by professional institutes and registration bodies.

Rules and regulations affecting architectural practices

- Architects Act 1997
- The Architects Code: Standards of Conduct and Practice (ARB 1999)
- Business Names Act 1985
- Capital Allowances Act 2001
- Civil Liability (Contribution) Act 1978
- Companies Acts 1985, 1989
- Consumer Protection Act 1987
- Contracts (Rights of Third Parties) Act 1999
- Copyright Designs and Patents Act 1988
- Data Protection Act 1998
- Disability Discrimination Act 1995
- Employers' Liability (Compulsory Insurance) Act 1969
- Employers' Liability (Compulsory Insurance) Regulations 1998
- Employment Acts 1980, 1988
- Employment Equality (Age) Regulations 2006
- Employment Protection (Consolidation) Act 1978
- Employment Relations Act 1999
- Employment Rights Act 1996
- Equal Pay Act 1970
- Fire Precautions Act 1971
- Fire Precautions (Factories, Offices, Shops and Railway Premises) Order 1976
- Health and Safety at Work etc. Act 1974
- Human Rights Act 1998
- Income Tax (Earnings and Pensions) Act 2003
- Income Tax (Pay As You Earn) Regulations 2003
- Income Tax (Trading and Other Income) Act 2005
- Insolvency Act 1986
- Limitation Act 1980
- Limited Partnerships Act 1907
- Limited Liability Partnerships Act 2000
- National Minimum Wage Act 1998
- Partnership Act 1890
- Pension Schemes Act 1993
- Proceeds of Crime Act 2002
- PII Guidelines (ARB 2001)
- Race Relations Act 1976
- RIBA Chartered Practice scheme – qualifying criteria
- RIBA Code of Professional Conduct 2005
- Sex Discrimination Acts 1975, 1986
- Supply of Goods and Services Act 1982
- Taxes Acts (updated annually)
- Trade Descriptions Acts 1968, 1972
- Unfair Contract Terms Act 1977
- Working Time Regulations 1998

Note: These are always liable to change and should be checked for currency.

Many of the regulations will be dealt with further in the sections on insurance, tax and premises, and in the various parts of the guide that cover employment issues, but it is worth considering at the early stages the framework in which you need to operate and how this affects your approach to starting up. Some regulations affect all business, regardless of size, but probably the greatest regulatory impact will be felt when you become an employer and you will need to be familiar with employment legislation before you take on your first

See also: Insurance, page 71; Tax, National Insurance and VAT, page 79, Premises, page 67

employee. Business regulation will tend to affect you more as the firm gets larger and the structure more complex, but there are plenty of regulations to trip up even the smallest firm.

It is rare that you will need to consult the original, primary legislation behind many of the statutory regulations, but you do need to know how they will affect you and your business, and you should maintain a watchful eye on new developments. Your advisers will help interpret in their areas of expertise, but it will be up to you to generally be aware and to stay up to date. If in any doubt, seek specialist advice.

Finances

A basic financial success rate is essential for survival, cash flow needs to be kept healthy and the overdraft kept under constant surveillance. Above this basic level of financial well-being you will have further goals, which might include levels of profit and income, investment and marketing expenditure, pro bono work and contributions to charity. Setting financial goals will involve the production of the kind of business plan your bank manager might recognise: involving profit and loss predictions, cash flow forecasts and analysis of the value of investments. A worked example is given in the box below, but many computer programs are also now available to help you with this; they can provide you with more sophisticated analyses and allow you to interrogate the information in various different ways.

Overheads

Your practice overheads will loom large in the debit column of both the financial forecasts and your budget so you will need to plan carefully for them. They will vary from the large, in particular staff salaries and premises and equipment costs, to the small, such as stationery, utility bills, etc. You can be fairly sure, however, that they will not have much relationship to activity level or, more especially, to income, as outgoings tend to be fairly regular and consistent while payments into your bank account will fluctuate wildly from month to month.

Investment early on in good quality, long-lasting premises, equipment and promotion may turn out to be money well spent – but only if you are successful. It can equally drag you down with unsustainable debt if you do not generate the income to support it. You need to assess and calculate the risks involved as part of your entire investment strategy – take advice if necessary to help with this and seek to compare your own with others' experience, if possible consulting any available benchmarking studies.

Despite taking advice and being cautious, it is easy to generate unnecessary overhead commitments early on. Invest in those parts of your business that are critical to your business plan and not elsewhere. Consider leasing equipment, at least at the start, and hiring staff only when you have work to give them and not before. Shared workspaces may provide you with many of the facilities you require at low cost and will allow you to grow your space requirements later on.

Financial forecast

Having spent time on researching your business objectives, the saleability of your own skills and services, the market, your USPs, the size and structure of your business, and so on; all this needs to be consolidated in a financial plan and a forecast of your financial needs, profits and losses. You are likely to need advice from a range of sources to achieve this and you should be aiming to end up with a short and fairly cogent financial forecast for up to the next five years. The forecast should show whether you need to raise capital to fund your business and, if so, how you will repay any loans. It should also provide the core evidence to convince a lender to provide you with that capital.

See also: Advisers, page 26; Professional advisers, page 76

As you start to run your business the financial plan should become a regular reference to guide your real performance, with targets both to achieve and to measure progress against. It must be reviewed and updated regularly as your true position becomes known, and any departure from the plan should provide you with adequate warning to take corrective action. Given the uncertain nature of architectural business a forecast of much more than a year is likely to be largely

Financial forecast – worked example

This fictional example of a financial forecast is for a five-person practice which has to grow to a six/seven-person practice by the fourth quarter to deal with a rapidly expanding workload.

Annual budget

	Jan–Mar £k	Apr–Jun £k	Jul–Sep £k	Oct–Dec £k
Receipts				
Fee income	32.5	41.1	113.2	84.2
Other (disbursements, rent charged, etc.)	0.7	6.6	8.1	8.0
Capital injection	0.0	0.0	0.0	0.0
Total receipts [a]	**33.2**	**47.7**	**121.3**	**92.2**
Payments				
Payments to creditors	0.0	(2.0)	(2.0)	(2.4)
Salaries/wages	(38.0)	(38.0)	(39.0)	(52.0)
Rent/rates	(6.0)	(6.5)	(6.5)	(6.8)
Insurance	0.0	(3.8)	(1.4)	0.0
Repairs and maintenance	(1.5)	(0.9)	(2.0)	(2.8)
Utilities	(0.3)	(0.3)	(0.7)	(1.4)
Postage/printing/stationery	(1.3)	(3.9)	(1.5)	(3.3)
Travel (including car expenditure)	(3.3)	(3.9)	(0.9)	(0.8)
Telephone and internet	(1.5)	(1.8)	(1.9)	(1.6)
Professional fees	(0.8)	(1.7)	0.0	0.0
Capital expenditure (equipment, etc.)	0.0	(5.8)	(6.0)	(1.2)
Interest/bank fees, etc.	(0.1)	(0.3)	(0.7)	(0.2)
Chargeable costs (job expenses)	(2.0)	(1.4)	(10.7)	(22.2)
Total payments [b]	**(54.8)**	**(70.3)**	**(73.3)**	**(94.7)**
Net cash flow [a – b]	**(21.6)**	**(22.6)**	**48.0**	**(2.5)**
Opening bank balance	**15.0**	**(6.6)**	**(29.2)**	**18.8**
Closing bank balance	**(6.6)**	**(29.2)**	**18.8**	**16.3**

Notes: Amount in bank at start of year is £15,000

Bracketed figures ( ) indicate a negative amount/outgoings

VAT inputs and outputs are not shown but can affect cash flow within the quarter speculative and not of great use, but treat six months as a minimum. This tends to result in a need to review and revise your financial plan about once a month.

Funding

Unless you have your own capital to invest in your new business, debt is likely to figure prominently in the first years of running the company. This will be a mixture of long-term debt with structured repayment and short-term borrowing to tide you through more immediate spending commitments. Some long-term debt may relate directly to acquisitions in the form of hire purchase agreements or other asset-based financing, with the debt secured against the equipment, but if you need to raise significant capital this is likely to be from a bank or a venture capital provider. The importance of having a bank to advise you has already been noted earlier in this work stage, but see also Work Stage F.

See also: Advisers, page 26, and Bank account, page 69

Company or trading name

You have done your groundwork, carried out market research, defined the services you plan to offer and developed financial forecasts. But you still need a name for your company (unless you picked this first and tailored everything else around it). This used to be easy – you took your own name or names and added an '& partners', and you had your brass plate made and put it up outside your door. Although this approach is still a popular option, it is only one among many others. With a more complex understanding of, and need for, branding in both the public and commercial worlds you will need to spend some time crafting, and possibly market testing, your proposed name.

Large commercial companies are well known for spending substantial sums on this aspect of their business and numerous naming and branding consultancies exist to fill the niche function of advising them. But there are a few basic considerations that should be taken into account when choosing your name. Branding in general is considered in more depth in Work Stage G.

See: Marketing, page 87

Naming your practice

When choosing what to call your business you will need to consider the name carefully:

- Is it a match for who you are? Pretending to be something that you are not is usually self-defeating.
- Why not use your own name(s)? This can be reassuring to clients and make marketing your practice more straightforward, as well as giving status to the named partners.
- Is it easy to pronounce?
- Is it easy to remember and is it memorable?
- Is it short and snappy or long and serious?
- Does it explain what the firm does or is it deliberately opaque or mysterious?
- Does it create an impression or impart a sense of style?
- Does it reinforce the vision you have for your company or obstruct it?
- Will it help make your company distinctive?
- Will it allow you room for flexibility or will it hem in your structure or product?
- Does it sound radical and provocative or solid and professional?
- Will you need to constantly explain it to enquirers?
- Does it mean something offensive, in English or any other language?
- Is it within the rules for company names? There are restrictions on the use of words such as 'National', 'Royal' or 'Institute'.
- Can it be combined with a logo?
- Will it produce variations for different purposes?
- Is there another company already using it (or something similar)? Check with Companies House (www.companieshouse.gov.uk).
- Has it already been registered as a brand name?
- Is a good internet domain name available for it? Check on www.nic.uk.
- When searched for on Google or other search engines, will it appear or will it be lost among other, irrelevant sites?
- Will you be happy announcing it every time you answer the telephone?
- Will it last or become rapidly dated?

Continued

This area is regulated under the Business Names Act 1985 – for further information see Companies House guidance booklet GBF3 (www. companieshouse.gov.uk).

Note: Sole traders and partnerships can operate under their own names or under another business name. But if you choose another title you need to put your own name(s) and business address on all your business stationery.

CHECKLIST

Work Stage D: The business plan

- ☐ Prepare a business plan for your proposed new venture, giving details of:
    - ☐ the company
    - ☐ business potential
    - ☐ your offer
    - ☐ promotion and marketing
    - ☐ business arrangements
    - ☐ finance.
- ☐ Seek out and appoint appropriate advisers, including your:
    - ☐ bank manager
    - ☐ solicitor
    - ☐ accountant
    - ☐ co-professionals.
- ☐ Identify through market research the sectors/clients you will working in/ for and targeting.
- ☐ Assess and be prepared to nurture your existing client base.
- ☐ Establish the services you intend to sell and a preliminary pricing structure. Ensure these are adequately saleable and distinctive in your chosen marketplace.
- ☐ Know how you will provide the services you will be offering for sale.
- ☐ Develop a marketing and promotions strategy that will bring you to the attention of the clients you wish to attract.
- ☐ Examine and decide on a legal structure for the company and carry out whatever preparations for this are necessary.
- ☐ Prepare financial forecasts and explore potential funding arrangements.
- ☐ Chose a name for your business.

Work Stage E
Running the business

This work stage concentrates on putting in place the procedures and systems to get your business up and running. It covers how to deal with managing, storing and retrieving a wide range of information and the working methods that you need to develop to help you run an effective and efficient business.

Once in place, office routines are often very difficult to change, at least not without great effort. A great many offices find themselves working in ways that were instigated at the establishment of the practice or were imported from firms that the founders had previously worked for. It is worth considering all office procedures with a view to importance, effectiveness and flexibility over time so that you can set up your practice in a way that will remain appropriate as the firm changes and develops.

Dealing with information

The company will receive and generate vast amounts of information; in many different formats and with content ranging from complete junk to vitally important. A carefully judged proportion of this information will need to be stored in such a way that it becomes a permanent and accessible record of the firm's dealings and a resource that will allow efficient working methods that reuse and improve on earlier efforts.

Filing and storing

At the outset, organising the general to and fro of information will not appear to be an issue; simple filing systems will seem adequate and memory a good way of finding material. Five or ten years later you will wish that you had been more rigorous from the start. This does not mean that you have to invest in elaborate document tracking software; rather, as you put items into files or longer-term storage you need to think about how you will retrieve them quickly when you need to. You should use a relatively standard method, one which will not rely on any one individual remembering where a particular item is located.

It is not unusual for clients to ring up years later asking for information about their buildings. You may have given them all the information in a maintenance manual, but now they have lost it. You are both their first and last port of call. Schedules of paint colours, specification information on equipment, planning consents and the mobile phone number of the original electrician will need to be retrieved quickly if you are going to maintain your reputation as fearsomely dedicated and efficient. File such information well now, so you do not waste hours looking for it later – if you can quickly produce the information for the client, they might even entrust you with another job.

The alternative view is that you should throw away all but the most essential information as having comprehensive sets of files only attracts legal attention and leaves you open to unwarranted fishing expeditions and, ultimately, claims. This may particularly apply to information generated by others; co-consultants, manufacturers, etc. Consider discussing the right level of information storage with your insurers as well as other advisers. Whatever level of information retention you decide on it will require constant vigilance to keep chaos at bay and prevent information overload, and it is only set to get worse.

The two primary categories of information you will need to store are:

• administration/practice related
• project related.

Keep them separate. From these two develop further cascading subsets for all the rest of your information. However, most of the material you receive in the office will fit into neither of these categories, and the great majority needs be to be put straight into the bin. Being ruthless with information from the start will serve you well, although the time taken sorting information into categories will take, and will continue to take, far more practice time than is reasonable.

Make sure that the two main storage methods, paper and digital, use a similar system of organisation and labelling, and that they back each other up as far as possible. Protect the key information (in whatever format) from fire, theft and damage – if necessary by using an off-site storage location. With digital infor-mation, storage media has a worryingly short life before being superseded by newer technology. Copy your old information onto new storage media as you upgrade, before the equipment to copy, or even to read, the information becomes obsolete. Remember that some of the information you hold will be confidential and commercially sensitive and needs to be treated accordingly. You should also ensure that you comply with the terms of the Data Protection Act 1998 and other European information regulations (further information is provided by the Information Commissioner's Office: www.ico.gov.uk).

Everyone knows about backing up information – in practice this is more observed in the breach. Develop at least a weekly or even a daily habit. File material regularly as well, if only to keep your work surfaces from being buried. If you keep paper files, then print out e-mails as well as copies of letters you send and file them too. If you intend to keep a paperless office you will need to be very rigorous and organised and you should seek further expert advice.

Keeping records

In the current business world, keeping records and maintaining an audit trail on decisions is an essential prerequisite of good practice; although note the comments above on keeping and recording only essential information – not everything should be kept, especially if it means that you might be held responsible for its accuracy or rightness.

Most architects have learned to carry a bound book in which they record their working lives; making notes of meetings and conversations, doodling and drawing sketch details, jotting down critical information and measurements, etc. These books should be treated like police notebooks and become part of your office records, labelled accordingly. They are the contemporaneous notes that you may later rely on in court. Some information will need to be copied across into job files, onto drawings or cross-referenced elsewhere in your filing system, but it all needs to be clear in its original form. Dates, times, names and positions should all be recorded, and information entered such that it will make sense on rereading years later, after you have forgotten all about it. The danger is that such notebooks can be full of enigmatic notes – useful briefly at the time, but unintelligible when you need to revisit them.

Make notes on every phone call, even those made on your mobile phone when you are out of the office. Much is said on the phone by way of advice to clients, instructions to builders, requests for action and information that needs to be remembered. Write it down as soon as you can, and if that is not feasible, request that the information is sent to you by e-mail or fax. Make it a habit from the beginning. It may take time, but it should also save you time when searching for bits of information later on. When you write down an address or phone number, also remember to transfer it to your main database, possibly with a note explaining who it is and their provenance and relevance. Hours can be spent searching old records for an important number or puzzling over the identity of someone unexplained mentioned in notes. Avoid the future frustration of knowing you wrote it down somewhere but being unable to put your hands on it.

Your record keeping should also include a record of your design thinking and decision making, especially any decision that has health and safety implications and for which there might have been several alternative solutions. This may be laborious, but it could prove more than worthwhile in any dispute, and it may even sharpen up your own thinking process.

Timesheets

Fill out timesheets. It may be yet another after-the-event item of record keeping that stops you getting on with the job in hand, but it can pay huge dividends in the longer term. The design of timesheets should be considered as part of the overall approach to developing standard office documents. Timesheets should record at least every half-hour of the working day, although some may be even more precise than that.

See also: Developing standards, page 58; Time management, page 118

Timesheets have a number of uses – they can provide:

- a general record of the work done on and the real-time programme of individual projects
- a record of the time spent on a job for billing and invoicing purposes
- information on the time spent on jobs that can be compared with the fees generated
- a means of comparing the amount of time spent on projects with targets (including financial targets)
- information on which to base future fee calculations, project programmes and job resourcing
- an overview of staff activity

- information on staff timekeeping and remuneration
- records for assessing staff efficiency and effectiveness
- the ability to balance fee earning activities with education, research, pro-bono work, professional activities, etc.
- a record of CPD carried out.

Computer software is available that will monitor individual activity and provide necessary prompts to supply information on activities that are not directly computer related, such as site visits, etc. These will automatically produce timesheets and job records and may be the best fit for your approach to practice. Alternatively, you may be happy to use self-generated spreadsheets or to fill out paper forms. Consider the options and pick the right method for you and your practice.

Accounting information

Keeping accounts for the purposes of HM Revenue and Customs is, of course, obligatory (more details are given in Work Stage F). But it can also help to keep your company financially astute and healthy.

See: Tax, National Insurance and VAT, page 79, and Keeping account, page 77

Like keeping track of the time spent on projects, knowing how the money is being spent and generated is important information for current and future planning. Information should be recorded in a format that will provide both historical data (the costs of running the practice and individual projects) and current data (which allow problems such as cash-flow crises to be predicted and, ideally, avoided). This will make job costing more accurate and allow calculation of fee proposals to be based on real information rather than rule-of-thumb percentages or, even, simple guesses at the costs of resourcing a project. Having access to reliable information in turn allows for better future planning and for deciding on matters such as monthly invoicing targets or overdraft requirements.

Knowledge management

As the practice develops it will also start to generate other forms of information and knowledge that you may want to record for future review, reuse and improvement. These might include:

- working methods and tools
- contact databases
- an image library
- templates for letters
- documents and forms
- standard details and palettes of products, materials, etc.

Develop ways of storing this information so that it can be easily located and accessed. Some information may need to be further adapted before use; if so, ensure that the original remains intact and track any changes that are made to it. The long-term storage methods for this information may be complex, and some larger practices have bespoke software to manage it electronically. If you plan to grow you may want to seek professional advice, but as a minimum use labelling and dating systems that enable efficient storage and will be searchable in the future.

Establishing the effective banking and use of such information may become the basis of a practice quality assurance system – whether called that or not – and, vitally, a means of knowledge management. Because architects are in the business of selling their knowledge – whether in the form of information or skill, expertise or judgment – managing your stock of knowledge is of great importance to your future prosperity.

Developing standards

A great deal of what architects do is the reinvention of solutions already explored and tested by themselves and others on previous projects. Whether you are writing a letter, preparing a document or designing and drawing a detail, consider whether you need to do it from scratch – or would it be more efficient to adapt an existing model? Alternatively, if you develop the item from the outset as a template for future use, you could make your practice more effective for the long term. This is common practice with standard contract forms and specification clauses, but it is less rigorously applied elsewhere in practice. Each solution needs to be customised for individual use, but maintaining a standards-based approach will, over time, allow for much more efficient practice and for the firm to grow in skill and understanding, based on previous experience.

Potential practice standards

Practice standards can be used in a range of applications, including:

- stationery, forms, etc.
- staff contracts
- bid material (staff CVs, project information, policy statements, etc.)
- appointment documents
- office management and project management letters (standard versions of these are also available from RIBA bookshops and others for adaptation)
- contract certificates and instruction forms
- specification clauses
- construction details
- images (drawings and diagrams, past projects, staff portraits, etc.)
- basic library
- material and product selection
- office manual/quality management system.

Practice library

The practice library was once at the heart of every architect's practice, occupying shelves of space supplemented by cupboards and boxes full of samples. For many practices this is still true, although internet access to the most up-to-date information has made it theoretically possible to operate without one. In addition, the restless pace of product obsolescence and development has added to the difficulty of maintaining a useful working library.

But develop it will, even if it is just to hold information on products and materials used on past projects and favourite publications that it is difficult to do without. But in order to be of use, the library has to be kept in good order. External library maintenance services are available, including individuals who may look after a range of office libraries, or commercial providers, such as the NBS Office Library Service from RIBA Enterprises, which offers a range of library services – from 'full maintained' to a 'core' library of the basic documents and reference texts for running a practice.

Library essentials

A vast amount of information can now be accessed via the internet, especially product and standards information. There are also internet-based services that offer, on subscription, expert systems of various types that guide users through the latest regulations, standards and products, etc. Other information may be available on CDs or in directories or binders. Some of the basics an office library might need to have available include:

- professional codes of conduct and guidelines
- planning information – including local plans and relevant Planning Policy Statements (PPS) documents
- Building Regulations and approved documents
- lists/references to British and European standard documents
- essential codes of practice
- Building Research Establishment (BRE) guides and notes
- practice and contract administration guides – e.g. *Architect's Job Book* and *Architect's Handbook of Practice Management*, standard letters in architectural practice, etc.
- practical information – e.g. *Metric Handbook* or Neufert (*Architects' Data*), detailing manuals, etc.
- urban design guidance – e.g. *Places, Streets and Movement* (ODPM), the *Urban Design Compendium* (English Partnerships) or *By Design* (CABE)
- relevant sectoral guidance – e.g. *Building Bulletins* (education) or the *BCO Office Fit-Out Guide*
- copies of standard forms of appointment and guidance for clients
- copies of standard contract documents
- specification information – e.g. NBS
- product selector compendia – e.g. *RIBA Product Selector* or *Barbour Index*)
- selected product literature and catalogues – and including the really useful such as the British Gypsum *White Book* or the Häfele catalogue
- a strictly limited range of product and material samples
- inspirational books and journals
- general reference books – including street maps, a dictionary and a thesaurus
- colour swatch books – including both BS and RAL colours
- tree identification guide.

Working methods

You may already have ways of working that you are more than happy with – but at the outset give your approach to work some thought to make sure that it:

- is or will be compatible with that of your partners, colleagues and employees
- is acceptable to your clients, colleagues and families
- maintains quality standards
- is safe, legal, fair and honest (i.e. professional)
- complies with your insurer's requirements
- will deliver the work programme on time and within cost
- permits your own and your colleagues' aspirations to be realised
- will provide the right mix of self-discipline and authority with relaxation and openness
- allows you, your colleagues and staff to have a good work–life balance.

As you start a practice, you are likely to be making the transition from employee to self-employed, or even employer. This requires a different attitude to work – including managing your own tendency to either over or under do it, as well as your ability to work with and to get the best out of others. The working style you adopt on day one of practice may stay with you for longer than you intended – start as you mean to go on.

Office policies

Some of your working methods may need to be expressed as formal or informal policies, possibly including an equal opportunities statement, a dress code or an approach to sustainability. Ultimately, these may be consolidated to form an office manual. Keep any office policy statements simple and short.

Timekeeping

Maintain reasonable working hours. Architecture has a reputation for a long-hours culture – but no business should expect to run on excessively long days. Quality of work suffers with tiredness. Late working should be the exception, and certainly not the rule – otherwise there is nothing kept in reserve for when it really is necessary.

Behaviour

Along with working methods will go working behaviour. What will be appropriate in the workplace, especially as you take on employees? Smoking is becoming less and less acceptable, or even possible, but other activities may also need policing or discouragement, including bad language, personal music players or private e-mail correspondence. At the beginning these may be dealt with individually, but as the company grows a written office policy may be needed. But as with so many matters arising in setting up and running an office it is always easiest to start as you mean to go on – so think and talk about these matters right at the outset so that you know where you are heading.

Internal communication

If you are setting up a single-handed practice then internal communication may not be high on your list of priorities, although you should make sure you have time out of job-focused activities to think about and plan the direction of your practice. For any larger firm a specific means of sharing information and ideas is essential. This might take the form of a regular weekly meeting or perhaps by having established tea breaks and meals together. Discuss what is coming up. Keep your colleagues involved in the development of the practice and use them to explore and test ideas and their presentation. But do not let the internal discussions overwhelm the running of the office or unnecessarily limit individuals' freedom of action.

Research

Design inevitably involves research, even if it is only to help make the choice between potential materials in a building. But it can be an essential part of a practice's approach to working and form an important element of the service offer to clients. Consider whether gaining new knowledge and information might be a significant part of your working method and how you would handle the results. Would it be for internal use only, for reporting to your client body or for more general publication and dissemination? Being a research-led practice might create wider opportunities, but also requires a more rigorous way of working.

Equipment

Your working methodology will be greatly influenced by the tools and equipment you use, and particularly by the computer system and the software you

See:
Equipment,
page 68

use on it. Choose equipment carefully to complement your preferred way of working – do not let your choice of working tools dictate your methods. Equipment requirements are discussed further in Work Stage F.

Training and CPD

Training and continuous professional development (CPD) are an obligatory part of a professional's working life, and the RIBA requires that all of its members do a minimum of 37 hours and gain 100 CPD points each year. This includes 17.5 hours from a set curriculum and an additional 2 hours of health and safety CPD. Professional CPD is ultimately the responsibility of individuals, but practices should also plan appropriate training for their staff and for the development of the practice. Training may vary from providing the practice with new and updated skills through to team-building exercises. The firm should ensure that one member of staff is responsible for CPD matters and that an annual plan for training and education is put in place and implemented.

Health and safety

Setting up a new company and taking on staff and premises brings with it responsibilities for the health and safety of you and your staff and for visitors. The extent of these responsibilities is beyond the scope of this guide, but you should ensure that you are aware of current health and safety legislation and take reasonably practicable steps to:

- ensure the health, safety and welfare of employees and others
- provide safe methods and places of work
- carry out appropriate risk assessments
- have measures in place to deal with emergencies and imminent danger
- provide appropriate protective equipment
- protect your staff when they are on site visits, etc.
- provide appropriate health and safety training for your staff.

Your responsibilities also extend to any formal role as Designer, as described in the Construction (Design and Management) Regulations (CDM), or other positions in a consultant team. These responsibilities can be onerous and need to be addressed as part of practice policy and CPD to ensure that you have appropriately qualified and knowledgeable staff.

As a practice you may want to put in place a health and safety policy that governs all these aspects of running a company. This can be done in-house, but an external health and safety adviser may bring more rigour to the process – the adviser may also monitor your performance and independently ensure your compliance.

If you or your staff will be visiting building sites as part of your working activities, then seriously consider qualifying for and obtaining a CSCS (Construction Skills Certification Scheme) card. Some sites will not allow you to visit without one. A minimum requirement for the card is a health and safety test run by the Construction Industry Training Board (CITB). For further information on the CSCS card see www.cscs.uk.com or www.citb-constructionskills.co.uk.

Further information on health and safety issues can be found in the RIBA's *Good Practice Guide: Employment,* and also at the Health and Safety Executive's website (www.hse.gov.uk) and through the Construction Industry Council's Safety in Design (SiD) initiative (www.cic.org.uk).

The RIBA Chartered Practice Scheme

The RIBA has established a scheme to help its members run more effective businesses and to ensure that the title Chartered Practice guarantees good standards of practice. The Chartered Practice Scheme will provide guidance and toolkits to member practices to assist with this. For further details see www.architecture.com.

CHECKLIST

Work Stage E: Running the business

☐ Develop a strategy for dealing with information – what to file and how and what to throw away.

☐ Get into the habit of recording (in a retrievable way) information, phone calls, decisions, etc. as they happen.

☐ Ensure that timesheets are kept by everyone in the company, accurately and usefully recording time spent.

☐ Develop an approach from the beginning that will generate and retain useful long-term knowledge for the business. Actively manage what the business knows.

☐ Develop standard solutions for a wide range of practice activities.

☐ The working methods of the business need to be appropriate and able to adapt for the long run. Do not just go with what you already know.

☐ Considerer developing office policies (implicit or explicit) on issues such as timekeeping, behaviour, research, training and health and safety.

Work Stage F
Setting up the business

Practical actions to be taken to establish the business and to put in place the support mechanisms for running it effectively and to help in any dealings with regulatory authorities.

Any work done in the preparation and establishment of a business plan should make putting that plan into action all the easier, but there are still a large number of practical actions to be taken – from the small-scale task of buying stationery to the major commitment of taking on premises.

The letterhead (graphic identity)

Deciding on the letter paper for the practice is in many ways a symbolic act of defining the existence of the new business. As well as giving factual information, such as listing the partners or directors or providing practical information, the letterhead should also give clues to other aspects of the firm, including the design approach of the practice and a feel for the spirit of the business.

The graphic identity that the letterhead contains should be echoed in other parts of the firm's identity – business cards and other stationery, the website, publicity, advertising, etc. Many architects see this as a challenge well within the scope of their creative abilities, but in general they are well advised to use a graphic designer to design it for them. This has the added benefit of experiencing how it feels to be a client of a design business.

Any graphic identity should be available to use electronically, possibly with a range of preformatted document templates. It may not be necessary to preprint all your stationery. Instead, use a laser printer to produce them as and when they are needed – the details on letterheads and stationery change relatively frequently and so this arrangement avoids wasted printing and permits ease of adaptability.

Business cards, however, should be printed and, despite their long history, are still the easiest and most popular means of exchanging business details. See your card as a small, and necessarily discrete, advertisement for your business, conveying a flavour of the practice's character and attitude to quality. There should be enough information on the card to explain itself without your presence – it must provide name, qualifications, postal, e-mail and web addresses, plus any contact phone numbers, including your mobile.

Standard items of stationery and graphic design

Items of graphic design and stationery for use in an architecture practice can include:

- company logo
- letterhead (including run-on sheets)
- letterhead for copy letters
- invoice headers (including copies, statements of account, reminders, etc.)
- order headers
- memo headers
- fax headers
- e-mail signatures and identities
- drawing issue sheets
- timesheets
- Architect's Instructions, etc.
- business cards
- compliment slips
- report cover sheets
- drawing title blocks
- standard 'project profile' sheets
- standard web pages.

Certain information must, by law, be included on letterheads and other documents (including business letters, orders for supply of goods and services, invoices and receipts, invoices and demands for payment). If you are operating as a sole trader or partnership the names of the owner or partners must appear either as part of the practice name or elsewhere. Partners or directors of LLPs or limited companies do not have to appear, but if you choose to put one or more on the letterhead then they all must appear. LLPs and limited companies must acknowledge that they are such and show the place of registration (England and Wales, Scotland, Northern Ireland or other specific variations) and their registered address and registration number. (For more details see Companies House guidance booklet GBF3: www.companieshouse.gov.uk.) If you are VAT registered then your registration number must also be shown on all invoices and receipts.

Premises

You do not need premises to set up in practice. Many architects' firms have been started at home, and many have remained there. But this is neither desirable nor possible for most firms and they will need to find a suitable property to lease or buy; to set up

See: Working at home, page 84

shop in. Not long ago this would have been a 'studio' space with good daylighting and plenty of space for drawing boards. Today, with most work being done at the computer or desk, you are more likely to be competing for space with other office-based businesses.

Premises location comparison (example)			
	Home office	Studio space	Serviced space	Purpose-designed office
Overheads	Minimal	Low	Medium	High
Rent/charges	None	Low to medium	High	Medium to high
Location	Potentially isolated	Out of the way/ difficult to access	Adequate	Good to excellent
Convenience	Good for sole trader	Low	High	Purpose-designed?
Facilities	Basic/small	Rough and ready	Good, if anonymous	As much as could be afforded
Public face	Poor	'Creative'	Adequate	Good to excellent
Growth potential	Poor	Good	Excellent	Limited
Resource sharing	Poor	Possible	Good	Limited

Selecting premises

Issues to consider when selecting premises may include:

- location and accessibility (for you, staff, clients and others)
- space and services
- style (what does the location and nature of the premises say about the firm?)
- image and public presence (do you want to show off your skills or have a street front?)
- costs (rent, rates, service charges, utilities, etc.) and any available grants
- scope for and cost of fitting out
- planning status
- location of your competition
- terms and length of lease
- health and safety
- security (for you and your staff and for your equipment after hours)
- scope for sharing space and facilities with others
- space for expansion or ability to reduce space required
- activity and behaviour of neighbours
- access to other facilities and local services
- relation to public transport
- car and bike parking.

Equipment

Your main working tool will undoubtedly be the computer, which will mean making an early choice between Windows, Apple Macintosh and other (chiefly Linux-based) operating systems and equipment. This guide is not the place to compare the pros and cons of these systems; you can easily find such comparisons elsewhere. Each of the systems has their fervent adherents and detractors, as well as many other users who would find either acceptable but have got used to one and would find it difficult to change. Most of the key programs run on either, but clearly Windows has the far greater range and choice, including of certain NBS products that are exclusively Windows-based. Note also that it will also shortly be possible to run the Windows operating system on Apple computers.

Some programs, such as Word, Excel, Photoshop and AutoCAD, have now become almost industry standards, and so if you choose to use alternatives you need to ensure that you can send and receive documents to and from everyone and anyone. Software, despite being an essential working tool, can also be a major expense, especially if a program is only rarely used. Look carefully to find the programs that suit the practice and only buy what you really need or can justify. Ensure you have appropriate licences for all the software you use and that it has been legally obtained.

Unless your office is very small, you are likely to need to connect your computers together with a central server, shared printers and other equipment. Seek specialist advice, as necessary, to get a robust working system – your ability to work will very quickly depend on the computer system reliably doing what it is supposed to. Ensure that you have maintenance agreements in place as necessary and know what to do if the system goes down.

A broadband connection to the internet is a necessity. If you use laptops a security protected wireless system can provide you with connectivity.

Other equipment you are likely to require includes:

- telephones (landlines, mobiles, organisers, etc.)
- printer (at least A3 format)
- fax machine (still useful, just, although can be replaced by a scanner/printer/computer combination)
- scanner
- photocopier
- digital camera
- measuring and surveying equipment
- drawing board(s) (despite the computers).

Bank account

It almost goes without saying that you will need a bank account. But this means choosing a bank, and this may require a great deal of consideration. Banks are competitive businesses like any other and you should at least expect them to be keen to have your custom. They also have a range of services to sell to you, which may or may not be appropriate or useful. Interview a range of banks to find the best for the circumstances and ambitions of your business. You need them to look after your money (and sometimes that of your clients), to offer

See also:
Advisers,
page 26

useful advice (see also the discussion in Work Stage D on the importance of your bank manager as business adviser), to provide overdrafts and loans and above all to stay with you and support you through good times and bad.

There is nothing to stop you having more than one account – but practicality dictates you will do most of your business banking with one bank, with whom you will want to build a good working relationship.

Choosing a bank

You should ask the following questions when interviewing potential banks:

- Does the bank take an ethical position concerning its business?
- Does it have a dedicated small business team?
- Does it have an understanding of the specific needs of an architectural business?
- Will your account be handled at a branch or at a regional level?
- Will you have a named senior contact at the bank?
- What access is there to business advisers?
- What are the qualifications and experience of the business advisers?
- What range of accounts is available?
- What range of services is on offer?
- What are the costs of those services?
- What arrangements are required for overdrafts/loans?
- What will happen if you experience financial difficulties (posit various scenarios)?
- What information will be required from you (and how frequently)?
- How are charges calculated – per transaction or a lump sum annual charge?
- What are the hidden charges – for example, for sending out letters?
- What telephone services are on offer?
- Are online banking services available?
- Will the bank try to sell you other, unrelated services?

Insurance

Theories of managerial economics tell us that profit is the reward for risk taking. While you will be in business to make a profit, you may not want to leave yourself completely exposed to all and any risk that the world may throw at you. This is where insurance comes in – it can be purchased to protect, variously, you and others, your work, your premises and your property. Some insurance may be legally required while other types are a matter of commercial choice.

Insurance requirements

Types of insurance that may be required by architecture practices include:

- professional indemnity (compulsory for practising architects)
- material damage
  - buildings and contents
  - computers
  - legal liabilities and costs
  - cash and securities
  - employee theft
  - personal accident
- liability
  - employer's liability (compulsory)
  - public liability
- travel
  - medical
  - accident
  - possessions
  - cancellation
  - delay
  - legal costs
- motor cars and driving
  - driver cover (third party liability compulsory)
- fire and extended perils
  - employer's liability (compulsory)
  - public liability.

Ensure that you have appropriate and adequate insurance to allow you to practise responsibly and to protect you and the practice should things go wrong. In all cases get professional advice on the types of insurance and levels of cover you require.

Professional indemnity insurance (PII)

PII is the minimum insurance necessary to practise as an architect, and the Architects Registration Board (ARB) requires minimum cover of £250,000 (for a fee income of less than £100,000 p.a.). PII will probably be one of your most significant business expenses and is likely to rise alarmingly (and occasionally fall modestly) from year to year. There is a range of brokers who specialise in arranging PII, ranging from large companies to smaller individual brokers. Each will have their advantages, as well as different approaches to providing you with specialist advice in the event of a claim or potential claim.

Talk to several brokers when you are seeking PII and get quotes from each. Ensure the insurance provided is in accordance with the requirements of the ARB and consider any other advantages each of the companies offers. Insurance is sold on a claims-made basis and a year at a time. This allows you to change insurers annually, but in order to maintain continuity and to establish a working relationship with your brokers you should plan to stay with one for the longer term. Consider the whole service on offer rather than simply the cost.

The ARB issues guidelines on PII requirements (see www.arb.org.uk). Note that the ARB views very seriously a failure to maintain appropriate PII.

A good insurer is likely to have a wealth of experience of the problems that architects come up against – make sure that you use their services to help manage your risks in practice. In particular, inform them as early as possible should you be concerned about a possible claim.

When filling out the proposal forms for insurers, ensure that you answer all the questions fully and accurately. Any non-disclosure of information may provide wriggle room for your insurer and leave you vulnerable to claims.

Note that the RIBA Insurance Agency (a division of a larger insurance broker endorsed by the RIBA) has a service specifically tailored to the needs of small practices. For further details see www.architectspi.com.

Choosing an insurer

When selecting an insurance policy provider, you should consider the following issues:

- compliance with ARB requirements
- limits to cover of liabilities (cover to be as wide as possible)
- insurance to be on the basis of any one or each and every claim
- legal costs to be included over and above any indemnity limits
- the quality of the claims service
- availability of advice
- wriggle clauses – avoid policies that attempt to use clever wording to evade liability or responsibility
- experience of provider
- and, only after considering everything else, cost.

Premises and contents insurance

It is important to cover yourself against loss and damage to both your premises and their contents. Consider how your practice would work should fire, flood or serious theft occur. The loss may not only be in terms of the costs of the physical material but also the often greater costs of reinstating systems to working order and retrieving vital archived material. Maintain and keep a good and up-to-date inventory of your property, equipment, stored material, etc. Aim to insure for complete reinstatement (new for old cover).

See also: Planning for disaster, page 131

Any equipment that is taken off the premises, such as laptops, cameras, etc. may have to be listed separately. Ensure that such lists are kept up to date as you buy, and retire, equipment.

Should you lease or rent your premises, insurance may come as part of the package. Ensure that any such insurance is appropriate for your needs and you are aware of the conditions attached to it. In such cases, contents insurance may have to be sought separately. Note that employees' and others' personal possessions may not be covered under the practice's insurance policies.

Beware of your insurer's subrogation rights. Once they have settled your claim they may seek to recover their loss from a third party. If your insurance (or lease) is held in the name of only one partner, the third parties might be taken to include other partners, employees, etc. Check that insurers waive their rights of subrogation against such parties.

Employers' liability insurance

The title of the Employers' Liability (Compulsory Insurance) Act 1969 (and the subsequent similarly named regulations) spells out the obligation on all 'employers' in business to have this insurance. There are some exceptions, including public organisations and family businesses that only employ close relatives, but it is generally applicable, and its existence is confirmed by the certificate of insurance that employers are obliged to display in an accessible position in their premises. Cover needs to be for at least £5 million, which covers costs of compensation for your employees' injuries and illnesses, whether they are caused on or off site, but excepting motor injuries. Further information can be obtained from the Health and Safety Executive, see www.hse.gov.uk.

Public liability insurance

Your employers' liability insurance only covers employees and not others who may visit your premises or could otherwise be affected by your actions. This is the purpose of public liability insurance. It is not compulsory but should be seriously considered, especially if you have a significant number of visitors or dealings with third parties.

Public liability insurance will cover you for damages awarded to a third party resulting from death or an injury to them or damage to their property caused by you or your business. It should also include related legal fees, costs and expenses. Policies vary, with many potential exclusion clauses and warranties – take specialist advice if you are considering taking out public liability insurance.

Health and accident insurance

Running a small business means that you are very dependent on your own, your partners' and key members of staff's health and ability to work. Considerable loss can result if any of you are unable to work through illness or accident. Personal accident, life and sickness insurance (as well as permanent health insurance) exists to cover this eventuality. It normally consists of lump sums to be paid out for various conditions and disablements, including death, loss of limbs or eyesight, etc.

Such insurance can be written for the benefit of the practice or the individual or a combination of both. It is different from private health insurance, which is aimed at paying for treatment. It should form part of the practice's overall strategy for dealing with risk and should be a potential part of employees' benefits packages.

Other insurances

Other insurances you may need to consider include motor and travel insurance and specialist cover for computers and other equipment.

Insurance advice

When seeking insurance generally you should:

- seek specialist advice
- assess the risks that you and the practice may face and seek appropriate insurance
- remember that it is better to take precautions and avoid unnecessary risks than to assume that the insurance policy will cover your loss
- keep inventories and adequate records, with copies in a safe place
- obtain alternative quotations through one or more brokers
- ensure that you, your personal assets and your practice are all adequately protected
- supply insurers with full and accurate information
- keep your insurers informed of changing circumstances
- inform your insurers, as soon as possible, of any circumstances likely to give rise to a claim (including the discovery of mistakes or claims by clients or others).

Professional advisers

Accountant

There is a common confusion between the activity of bookkeeping and the role of the accountant. You (or your bookkeeper) should expect to compile all the information on your income and outgoings and understand enough about the workings of the accounts to know where you stand at any point.

See: Keeping account, page 77
Indeed, if your accounts are simple and straightforward you will not need the services of an accountant at all – you can get HM Revenue and Customs to calculate your tax liability and pay it accordingly.

If you need to get an accountant to take your bills and invoices and make sense of them you are probably being unnecessarily profligate. Although your accountant may check the books and straighten them out to comply with accounting standards, present them to HM Revenue and Customs and calculate the amounts due, that is not their main role or advantage to you. Their job is to act as your business adviser and help to make sure that the financial side of your business is running as effectively and efficiently as possible and that you are complying with the requirements of the law in doing so. You need to choose an accountant who is sympathetic to your business needs as well as being reliable and knowledgeable. They must be someone to whom you would feel happy to turn as and when necessary.

Public relations consultant

You may have a natural flair for relations with the media and be able to generate your own publicity, but the likelihood is you will not have the time or the expertise. A PR consultant may not be an early, or even an essential, appointment. However, if you do want to develop the profile of your new business early on, or perhaps even start with an attention-grabbing launch, then the advice of a PR consultant will prove invaluable, and it may prove very helpful in the longer-term success of your practice.

If you are considering choosing a PR consultant, do your research and explore with a variety of potential companies or individuals how you can work together – what, in practical terms, you might get out of it and how much it would cost. It is likely that you will need someone with specific experience of the architectural/design sector, who knows the appropriate journalists and others to suggest to you or to contact on your behalf. Such experience is also likely to bring an aware-ness that budgets for PR in architecture are modest at best, and to know how to make them stretch accordingly.

Solicitor

Every so often you will need the skills of a lawyer, whether to prepare a deed of partnership, read through a proposed contract, write a formal letter to a client to chase an unpaid invoice or do property conveyancing. It is worthwhile establish-ing a relationship with an individual solicitor who can help you for the majority of your needs and can provide general legal and business advice. But should you require specialist legal assistance, for example in construction law, you should seek out a lawyer with the appropriate skills and knowledge in that sector of the law.

RIBA Members' Information Line

The RIBA offers a members' information helpline (tel: 020 7307 3600, fax: 020 7361 1802), which can provide access to a panel of specialist practice advisers for help and guidance on a range of practice issues – from legal and contractual problems to taxation or planning advice. Further details are given on the 'library/informa-tion services' pages at www.architecture.com. The RIBA also has a specialist legal support service, which can provide advice on employment, human resources and health and safety matters. For details see the employment practice page of the RIBA website: www.architecture.com.

Keeping account

The demands of running any business mean that an excessive amount of time is spent keeping accounts in order; recording money spent and earned, sums owed and owing and amounts invoiced and paid. And although it is an essential part of ensuring the business survives and is successful, it is unlikely that you started the practice with any appetite or enthusiasm for the exacting and time-consuming activity of recording every single transaction you make.

It may sometimes appear that the only reason for keeping such records is to satisfy HM Revenue and Customs that you are paying the correct amount of tax and VAT. However, it does have a useful side: it provides an essential financial management tool that allows you to maintain control of your profitability and cash flow and to monitor the success, or otherwise, of your business strategy.

Accounting practices and procedures have developed to use your accounts to help you with this and to produce reports that give an insight into the health and prospects of your practice.

This guide is not the place to deal with the inner details of accounting practice – those are readily available elsewhere – but it does look briefly at some basic principles of keeping the books and making sense of them. Much bookkeeping work is now handled by computer programs, which have greatly eased the keeping of accounts, but you should still be familiar with the underlying approaches.

A number of systems will be available to you and you should aim to use the simplest that is applicable to both your business and your accountant, now and into the future. Consider setting up your own spreadsheet program if that is all you really require – at least you will thoroughly understand it. If you are starting a single-handed practice and have no great ambition to expand, avoid an elaborate system designed to deal with the workflow of large numbers of staff and individual profit centres. Alternatively, if you do plan to expand, look for a system capable of coping with a greater number of tasks and more complex analysis of results.

Single-entry bookkeeping

The most basic system is a single-entry procedure, which can easily be done on paper or on a simple spreadsheet. This involves recording each item of income (receipts) or expenditure (payments) in its own row, with the columns separately recording the date, name and unique reference number of the transaction, details and amount. Totalling the columns will give you a simple cash flow in and out and a balance between the two. This is, more or less, how your monthly bank statement is presented to you, and if the dates correspond, they should result in the same sums. The information from this will allow you to put together a simple profit and loss account for each period.

See:
Financial
forecast,
page 48
A more developed version of this system breaks down the details column into subcategories, such as 'travel', 'utility costs', 'rent', etc., as was illustrated with the example financial forecast given in Work Stage D, and each of these is then given its own 'amount' column or ledger. This allows the totals to reflect the different types of expenditure and income over a period and gives you a greater, at-a-glance

understanding of where the money is being spent or earned. Your profit and loss account can now be developed into something more useful for management purposes.

If your business is VAT registered, the VAT paid should also be recorded in separate columns. The resulting totals will provide a simple assessment of VAT to be paid at the end of your accounting period.

In order to check your accounts you will need to reconcile them against your monthly bank statements, taking into account any unpaid invoices, uncashed cheques or monies that you may owe. Any mistakes that have crept in will have to be flushed out – sometimes a laborious process. Single-entry book-keeping is a good, robust system for a small business without too many transactions, but it will not, by itself, help you reconcile your accounts or flag up unpaid bills, etc. For this, accountants long ago developed a more complex and fiendish procedure.

Double-entry bookkeeping

The double-entry system is the method used by accountants and professional bookkeepers and is so called because each transaction is recorded twice over; once for value given and once for value received. It records the exchange of goods or services for money, transaction by transaction. The balance between total value received against total value given at any time will reveal the financial state of play. Ultimately, once all bills are paid, the balance should be zero.

The double-entry system may be complex but it is very well suited to computer systems, which can straightforwardly transfer and cross-refer information from one area of data to another. Assess the different packages that are available and discuss suitability and compatibility issues with your accountant before making a choice.

Tax, National Insurance and VAT

Tax planning

As you go into business you are going to work for both yourself and the Government. HM Revenue and Customs has an interest in your taxable revenue and uses you to collect VAT on its behalf. In order to deal most effectively with this you need to plan your tax so that you pay only the most advantageous rates and amounts of tax, you have the resources to make the payments when the time

---

Terminology: double-entry bookkeeping

Double-entry bookkeeping has its own strict terminology:

- the receipt of value creates a *debit*
- the giving of value creates *credit*
- transactions are recorded in a *set of books,* comprising *day books* or *journals* and *ledgers*
- entries are made in the day books or journals; these include a general journal plus more specific journals such as a cash book, sales book and purchase book (each recording the transactions under a number of headings as with the single-entry system)
- the information then is transferred, or *posted*, to individual *ledgers* that deal with specific accounts.

Information can be drawn from both journals and ledgers to provide detailed assessments for the financial management of the company, including cash flow, invoice chasing and the identification of waste. Ultimately, your debit total (comprising assets and expenditure) should equal your credit total (comprising liabilities and income).

See: Company structure, page 37

comes and you do so at the very last moment. Tax planning will certainly affect your choice of company structure (see Work Stage D) and is something you need to address in detail with your accountant right at the outset of starting your business.

HM Revenue and Customs offers a free face-to-face business advice service from their Business Support Teams to those starting up a business. It also publishes guidance booklets, such as *Starting for yourself – The Guide* (2005), to help you through the tax system. See www.hmrc.gov.uk/startingup for more details.

Income tax

Income tax is the responsibility of individuals to pay, and if you are going to be a partner or a director in the business you will need to ensure that you complete your tax return in the usual way, deducting any allowances. Income tax, together with national insurance, is paid half yearly on the 31st of January and July, based on an assessment of the previous year's figures. You need to register with HM

Revenue and Customs for both income tax and National Insurance when you start out on your own. If you are starting as a sole trader or as a partner, your tax status will be updated to that of self-employed, although if you are gaining income from more than one source (for example from teaching) then you may still be taxed directly by your other employer(s).

Your taxable income will be calculated as the amount remaining once you have deducted from your total income any allowable expenses resulting from running the business. You should seek advice as to which expenses are allowable, particularly if you are working from home or other premises where some expenses may be shared.

See also: Capital allowances, page 82

If you have, or plan to have, employees you will also be responsible for calculating and collecting their income tax through the Pay As You Earn (PAYE) scheme. Again you will need to register with HM Revenue and Customs, and you will be issued with the information and facilities to carry this out.

National Insurance

National Insurance is collected on top of income tax, either as part of employment (Class 1 contributions) through PAYE, or, if you are self-employed, through both Class 2 and Class 4 contributions. Class 2 contributions are collected at a flat weekly rate, usually by direct debit, and entitle the contributor to incapacity benefit, the basic pension, widow's benefit and maternity allowance. Class 4 contributions are collected along with income tax payments at a rate based on a fixed percentage of income between set lower and upper limits. They carry no further entitlements.

A self-employed person is obliged to notify HM Revenue and Customs within three months of their new status. If you have other employment it is likely you will be required to pay Class 1, 2 and 4 contributions as appropriate.

Corporation tax

If you have set up as a limited company then the company will pay corporation tax on its profits in each financial year. The taxable profit is the sum of the cash profit at the end of the year plus the value of any dividends that you and your fellow directors may have paid yourselves. Corporation tax is payable by the end of December following the year in question – ensure you have enough money set aside to cover this payment.

Capital allowances

Some purchases cannot be directly set against income within a single tax year – instead, the capital value has to be written off year by year as the value depreciates. This applies to items of plant, computer equipment, vehicles, etc. Various allowances apply and small businesses may have special allowances. These will need to be checked; but normally value is written off at 40 per cent in the first year and 25 per cent thereafter.

VAT

Value Added Tax (VAT) is a sales tax levied on goods and services, which you add to your invoices. It is then repaid, by you, to the VAT office of HM Revenue and Customs. Unlike other taxes your business only has to register for VAT once your 'taxable turnover' exceeds a certain threshold (currently £60,000).

As your business grows you will need to decide when to register for VAT. There are clear advantages to your clients if you are not yet VAT registered, and it may also mean less paperwork for you. But passing on your VAT payments through your invoice system can benefit your business, and many businesses will decide to register early for the level of respectability that VAT registration can bring.

VAT on architectural services is generally charged at the standard rate of 17.5 per cent, which will include the cost of any other expenses or disbursements you are charging for, whether fully rated or not. This is described as the 'output tax'.

VAT is usually accounted for and paid quarterly, but if your taxable turnover is less than £660,000 you can join the annual accounting scheme and report and pay yearly. Staying below the same limit also permits you to use the cash accounting scheme, which allows you to pay VAT only once you have been paid yourself, a facility that can significantly aid cash flow.

If your business has paid out VAT when paying for running expenses you can reclaim this 'input tax' when preparing the VAT account (although there are some exceptions, such as entertainment expenses and buying cars). However, note that some of your purchases may not include VAT and on others it may only have been charged at 5 per cent. If your input tax exceeds your output tax in an accounting period you will be repaid the difference, but only if the business is VAT registered. The VAT account is prepared on a standard form supplied for the purpose and needs to be submitted with payment, if applicable, within one month of the end of each accounting period. A VAT account can also be submitted and paid online.

Recognising that the preparation of quarterly, or even annual, VAT accounts is onerous for very small businesses (although it also provides a very useful discipline for other accounting procedures), HM Revenue and Customs runs a flat rate scheme. If your taxable turnover is less than £150,000 annually, the scheme allows payment of VAT at a standard rate of 12.5 per cent (depending on sector) of taxable turnover. Assess whether this is advantageous to you before applying.

Other taxes

Other taxes may also apply to the business, such as capital gains tax, vehicle excise duty and a TV licence. Consult your accountant, especially if your interests extend overseas or into unusual areas of business.

Self-assessment

Under the self-assessment system individuals and companies are responsible for recording their taxable business activities and calculating and paying the amounts due on time, regardless of whether they have been sent reminders or the correct paperwork and forms. Fines and interest payments may be levied if this is not achieved.

Pensions

Consider pensions for the partners or directors and for others as part of your long-term tax planning – seek specialist advice.

You should also note that if you have more than five employees you are likely to have to offer them access to a stakeholder pension scheme. For more details see www.pensionsregulator.gov.uk.

Working at home

One of the great advantages of being self-employed is that you can work at home, although this is clearly not suitable for everyone. You should consider the following pros and cons before deciding to set up your business in your own home:

Pros

- Low overheads
- Short commuting time
- Flexible working hours
- Good/comfortable working environment
- Informality
- Fluidity between work and home life
- The use of house as showpiece

Cons

- May need planning consent
- The possible need to pay business rates may change the nature of your property
- Never being able to leave the office at the end of the day and a lack of separation between life and work
- No 'orientation time' gained during the journey to work
- Distractions (from family, friends, housework, etc.)
- Need for self-discipline
- Professional isolation and loneliness
- Lack of formal reception or meeting rooms
- Invasion of privacy
- Need for perpetual tidiness
- Perception of a lack of seriousness
- Loss of space in the home
- Difficulty of expanding or providing space and facilities for staff

If you do decide to work at home you should consider the following actions, which may help you to run your business effectively:

- Maintain separate office and home spaces, even if adjacent

Continued

- Ensure you have appropriate insurance and that your insurers understand the work/home arrangement
- Have separate home and office telephone systems/numbers
- Use a telephone answering service
- Set firm times for work; and 'go home' in the evening
- Use meeting facilities elsewhere for critical meetings
- Establish locum and job sharing arrangements with co-professionals
- Establish regular social and professional links with other small businesses and built environment professionals, including participating in RIBA activities and CPD events
- Take proper holidays.

CHECKLIST

Work Stage F: Setting up the business

☐ Commission a graphic identity; including letterheads (and other stationery and e-mail) and web page design templates. Resist the temptation to do it yourself.

☐ Think through where to have your office premises. Your choice will communicate a lot about you and the practice. It will affect how and how well you will work and the quality of your life (or lives) as well as your ability to attract high-quality employees.

☐ Choose your equipment with care, especially computer and software systems – they can be very difficult to change later.

☐ Select your bank with care – shop around before making your choice.

☐ Make sure you are adequately insured, including both those insurances you must have to practise legally and those which protect you and the business from undue financial risk should the unexpected (but predictable) happen.

☐ Appoint and consult professional advisers who can help you protect your business and make it a success.

☐ Keep full and proper accounts and make the information work for the practice as well as for HM Revenue and Customs.

☐ Plan effectively to minimise your tax exposure. Know what taxes are due and make sure that you have the resources in place to pay them when they become due.

Work Stage G
Getting noticed

You have set up your practice on the basis of a solid business plan and you are ready for the launch. You may even already have some work to get the new venture underway. But you will need to find new clients and projects in order to develop the practice and keep it going. Who are they and where are they going to come from?

Marketing

In comparison with many businesses, architects' clients are a particularly diverse group – they can be practically anyone, any group or any business. You could even be your own client. It can therefore be a difficult group to target, but it is essential to do so if you are going to spend what will be a very limited marketing budget wisely. In establishing your business plan you will have decided to concentrate on certain sectors, and they will be your main focus, but there are also some other basic ways in which you should make yourself known.

In addition to adopting a broad-brush approach, you need to target specific areas that your intelligence gathering has indicated will be likely sources of work. Ensure you have enough information about the sector, or possibly subsector, to make yourself incisive and useful to a client and to show them that you can be of practical help. You are in the business of selling them a problem-solving service; you need to persuade them that the skills you have on offer are a close fit for the ones they believe they need.

Clients will be interested in whether you have or have access to the resources necessary to supply their needs. A good track record may be enough to satisfy them that you can handle their project, but you might also be expected to show that you have a team of staff, consultants and possibly suppliers and contractors readily available to realise their vision. The expectations of clients and the reality of resourcing projects are frequently poles apart, and this can be a significant problem for new and small practices. You may have to find ways of creatively responding to this

Marketing: the basics

Existing contacts	Stay in touch with your existing clients and contacts. Word of mouth and personal recommendation is the most effective means of getting work.
Website	Even if it is only a single page announcing your existence and listing your e-mail address and phone number, you need to have a web presence.
Directories	Make sure you are in the Yellow Pages and any other appropriate directories, both printed and online; especially if the listing is free.
RIBA	Use the RIBA Client Services recommendation service. Submit information and images. Keep information up to date.
Literature	Have at least a printed sheet publicising your practice to hand out or send out.
Networking	Go to events and meet people, including colleagues and potential clients.
Press and media	Make contact with journalists, submit regular press releases and news stories, write letters, articles, etc.
Exhibitions	Participate in exhibitions and architectural marketing events.
Events	Organise activities as part of events such as Architecture Week. Open your practice for public visits and get your buildings included in events such as Open House.
Surgeries	Participate in Architect in the House/Office events or hold architectural surgeries at other times or during other events.
Groups and clubs	Become active in local groups and activities, whether connected with architecture and design or not.
Pushiness	Being shy and diffident never won any work.

in order to persuade clients that your modest size practice can deal with their modest size job, even though it is very large and very important in their eyes.

The RIBA's Chartered Practice Scheme enables qualifying practices to promote themselves in both the printed and on-line directories that the Institute produces as well as through RIBA Client Services' nominations and exhibitions activities. The RIBA also organises events such as Architect in the House that put architects in touch with potential clients. For further information see www.architecture.com or telephone 020 7307 3725.

Beware of corporate brochures. These cost large sums of money, date very quickly and are difficult to know what to do with. Most clients will be able to get everything they need to know from your website. You can always produce a postcard to act as a physical reminder or advertisement for your website – it is much cheaper to produce than a brochure.

Websites are becoming more critical in the selection of architects by potential clients. As well as being a form of advertising and promotion and a source of information about the practice: clients and their advisers are using websites extensively to vet architectural firms and draw up shortlists. Ensure that your site is not only attractive and easy to navigate, but that it also provides the information that clients might be looking for, and in an easily printable form. The content is there for the clients – not for you.

Sending out targeted mailshots and cold-calling is always a possibility, but targeting should be fairly precise and any leads need to be rigorously followed up. It is likely that there are better ways to expend your energies pursuing work. The story with regard to advertising is similar – do it for the goodwill and for keeping the practice in the public eye but do not expect it to show immediate payback in the form of worthwhile work. A three-year time lag between publicity and any resulting paid work is considered an approximate norm. Always put yourself in the shoes of the recipient of your mailshots/calls/ advertising and imagine what would convince you to appoint someone you had never heard of before.

Respond to advertisements placed in the architectural press and elsewhere from clients looking for architects. They may not happen very often, but can be very well worth pursuing, particularly if you fit a particular age or geographical require- ment and can act immediately. But do not hold your breath for a successful or immediate result, and avoid excessive investment in preparing materials.

All marketing data support the notion that your best customers are the ones you already have – so look after them and ensure that you continue to give them a good service long after their project has been delivered and they have paid their final invoice. Almost all happy clients will return in due course with more business. They are also your best sales force – they can recommend you to a wide range of their contacts and they can provide useful references and reassurances to future clients. Cherish them.

Publicity materials

To help you in your marketing effort you need evidence that:

- you are who you say you are
- you have qualifications, experience and a track record
- your practice matches clients' aspirations.

Such evidence will help to provide reassurance to a client that the risk they are considering taking on in appointing your practice is minimal. It can take many forms: from yearly accounts and details of insurance to glossy photos of previous projects and glowing testimonials. You need to have it ready to be assembled into a format that meets the requirements of the moment. The same material, in different forms, will be needed to do many different jobs, from providing copy for magazine articles to filling out complex pre-qualification questionnaires (PQQs).

Overcoming procurement barriers

A constant concern for new practices is how to obtain work from mainstream clients, particularly those in the public sector. New procurement systems, attitudes to risk avoidance and the common requirement to demonstrate extensive prior experience with similar projects all place considerable barriers in the way of winning such work. It may take time and commitment to gain such work, but it is not impossible – even for the very smallest of practices.

Small-scale work

Many public bodies have a requirement for consultants to deal with the myriad of very small projects, repairs, refurbishments, etc. that they have to handle. It is not glamorous work and may not pay well, but it would allow you to get a foot in the door and gain that valuable experience and client base. Alternatively, it is possible to build up experience by working directly for individual organisations that operate under a local authority umbrella, such as schools and community centres.

The evidence

Evidence of your professional competence and successful track record can take many forms:

- Presentation drawings and sketches – whether drawn up before or after construction, can become very useful publicity material.
- Photographs – the opportunity to get good images of your projects is often short lived. Use professional photographers as far as possible – they can be eye-wateringly expensive, but are worth it in the long run.
- Client testimonials – best obtained when the client is most enthusiastic about the service you have provided. They may not have an obvious or immediate use, but once you have them they can be drawn upon whenever appropriate. Also collect positive comments from others, including planners, politicians, funders, users and visitors.
- Press coverage – buildings can attract considerable amounts of media interest, and some coverage can be very usefully reproduced in your and your clients' favour. Media appearances may also be useful, although more difficult to reproduce.
- Awards – there are awards schemes for every conceivable aspect and type of project. Enter awards – they are a very convincing recognition of your practice's quality and acceptability, and some can provide real kudos.
- Books – the publishing industry produces huge numbers of books on architecture and interior design, many of which will need illustrations and case studies. Publications vary enormously in quality, but being featured indicates professional standing and will please clients.
- Exhibition catalogues and directories – more evidence of your standing.
- Competitions – successes and shortlistings, or possibly succès d'estime, can only enhance your reputation, but take care who you show your more outlandish ideas to.
- Writings – published articles and papers are all evidence of your credibility, especially if they show in-depth knowledge of a relevant subject area. A book in your own name will take this even further.
- Research – research developed and published can be very useful evidence of active and informed involvement in an area, especially if immediately appropriate to a particular project. It may also lead to other strands of business activity.

Continued

- Company profile – information on the practice tailored to different audiences and different lengths. It may take the form of sheets that can be bound or distributed with project sheets, staff CVs, etc. Keep the information up to date.
- Project sheets – sheets giving succinct details of each project carried out by the practice, or by practice members in previous jobs and roles. Project sheets should be branded and have a consistent graphic identity and layout, and may be bound together for a bespoke document, made available on the web, etc. Prepare a new sheet immediately following completion of each project.
- Staff CVs – an important shot in your locker is the experience of the partners, directors and staff, as well as other consultants to the company. Keep these up to date and adaptable to different circumstances.
- Roles and appointments – in addition to the staff CVs, you may wish to highlight certain skills or appointments within the practice, such as conservation or planning qualifications, academic positions or advisory roles in relation to companies, government or institutions.
- Project list – a database of past and current projects, cross-referenced to allow you to produce suitably tailored selections of projects.
- Client list – a record of your past and current clients and the projects you have carried out for them. Ensure that you have each client's consent before releasing any information about them.
- Annual accounts – frequently requested in PQQs or credit applications, etc. Maintain in a form that you are happy to release for external scrutiny.
- Bank reference – also a PQQ requirement. Maintain an up-to-date version.
- Insurance documentation – most insurance companies supply certificates of insurance for issuing to potential clients, etc. Otherwise, ask your insurer what information they permit you to reveal.
- Quality assurance – documentation of the practice's quality assurance procedures and evidence of relevant accreditation, such as RIBA Chartered Practice status or Investors in People.
- Registration information – information on company, VAT and data protection, etc. registration.
- Practice policy statements – might include health and safety, equal opportunities or environmental statements.

Specialist work

If your practice can supply a specialism that is in sufficient demand and without an adequate supply it will give you a way in to obtaining work with a range of otherwise difficult-to-reach clients. Such skills in the past have included: off-site and modern methods of construction, cladding, public consultation and the realisation of public art works and projects.

Approved lists

In order to get work from large or public sector clients it is probable that you will first need to apply and then get onto a pre-vetted preferred suppliers list. Contact local authorities, etc. to discover who maintains such lists and the criteria they apply in selection for them. There will also be a number of other hurdles to overcome:

- Each local authority requires different information and a different set of forms to be filled in.
- Many public bodies require that you are pre-registered with and vetted by Constructionline, a register of construction-related contractors and consultants run on behalf of the Department of Trade and Industry (DTI). There is an annual fee to pay, which is based on number of staff (for one to five staff it is currently £70 plus VAT). For more details see www.constructionline.co.uk.
- Many public bodies require a professional indemnity insurance level of £5 million. This is far more than many practices carry, and more than is appropriate for the small-scale work that falls below the European Union (EU) value threshold.

Supply2.gov.uk portal

The Government has recognised the problems faced by smaller firms in accessing public sector work. One response has been to launch a portal for lower-value contracts (under £100,000) to provide better ways for small to medium-sized enterprises to bid for work that falls below the OJEU threshold (see *OJEU notices*, below). For further details and to register see www.supply2.gov.uk.

Frameworks supply teams

The next step up from being placed on a list of approved suppliers is to become a framework supplier. This might be beyond the reach of a recently established practice, but a bid in which the practice is part of an integrated supply team of contractors, suppliers and consultants with enough credibility would stand a far greater chance of success.

OJEU notices

Many practices subscribe to the *Official Journal of the European Union* (OJEU) and respond to advertisements for architects' services that are placed there for work across the EU. All public projects with a lifetime contract value greater than approximately £154,000 are required to be advertised in the OJEU. However, there is a poor record of small to medium-sized architectural practices winning work from this source. The website www.ojeu.com provides a free daily highlights reporting service on OJEU notices. For more information see the publication *Introduction to the EU Procurement Rules*, available from the Office of Government Commerce website www.ogc.gov.uk.

Advisory work

With the increase in complexity of procurement systems, many clients – especially in the public sector – are requiring client-side advice on feasibility, consultation, procurement and briefing. Such opportunities make it possible to work on large-scale projects without the resource implications of developing designs to detail design stage. However, this work does require a considerable degree of experience and expertise and a good understanding of clients' procurement needs. The RIBA runs an accreditation system for Client Design Advisors; for further details see http://members.riba.org/clientdesignadvisor.

CHECKLIST

Work Stage G: Getting noticed

- ☐ Have a marketing strategy and put it into action.
- ☐ Ensure that you have covered the basic and straightforward means that will get you noticed and that allow you to be found by someone not looking overly hard.
- ☐ Make sure you have a website with your basic contact details.
- ☐ Pay attention to your existing clients and contacts. Looking after them will show far more results than chasing after new and unknown leads.
- ☐ Compile (in advance) the evidence to show potential clients, use for publicity, etc. Maintain it in a standard format that can be quickly assembled for specific uses.
- ☐ Find ways of getting the kind of experience that is called for in your target sectors. Be ingenious and creative if needs be.
- ☐ Get your practice on approved lists, attached to consortia, in supply teams and into frameworks.
- ☐ Respond to advertisements and calling notices looking for architects and architectural services.
- ☐ Sell yourself hard – no one else will.

Work Stage H
Winning work

Getting noticed and shortlisted by potential clients is possibly half the battle, but you still have to win the appointment, potentially beating several equally well-qualified competitors. The appointment process is rarely immediate and usually involves a period and process of negotiation, sometimes including a decision on how much work to do at risk and without a proper agreement. It can also be a time to decide whether the client is one you would prefer not to become further involved with, and to make your excuses and back away.

Winning work

The ability to convince complete strangers that you are the right architect for them and their project is a skill that some appear to have naturally and others struggle with, but it is critical for the success of your business. If you are not a natural then it may be wise to seek training in presentation, interview and negotiation techniques.

Working at risk

Many clients will expect you to work for them for free – at least initially. How much is expected will vary from a first discussion about a project, when they will want to hear your preliminary ideas, to taking a project right up to planning consent – with many different degrees between. How far you are prepared to go along with this is a business decision, and so is up to you. Clients, not unreasonably, will accept what is on offer. You may feel that you have no choice and that all your competitors are doing it, but you may also find that many clients respect the value of a service that is charged for more than one that is given away for nothing.

Consider in advance how much you are prepared to offer at risk to get started on a project. Ideally have a firm practice position on unpaid work. You will find it much easier to stick with and to explain to clients if it is an across-the-board policy, and they will feel that they are being treated the same as everyone else. Many practices charge for all preliminary work at a flat hourly rate and do not find it a problem. Certainly it may not do your bid a lot of good if you are seen as too desperate to get the job or too much of a pushover in a negotiation.

Competitions, although popular with new practices, should be seen as being in this category, although some practices have built very successful businesses on the back of them. Calculate your reasons for and the benefits of entering competitions before putting often considerable resources into them. The reasons for entering may extend well beyond the prize of winning an important job – the practice may also benefit from the potential publicity and exposure, experience and team-building that undertaking such projects brings. But be certain why you are doing it, over and above the excitement of the gamble of the competition itself.

Success in interviews

Make sure that you can perform at introductory meetings and formal interviews – practice if necessary. Consider issues such as:

- background research/knowing your stuff
- dress
- punctuality
- establishing rapport – charisma is important
- picking the right approach for the interviewer(s)
- body language, handshakes, smiling, eye contact, posture, etc.
- maintaining a positive attitude – self-belief and confidence are essential
- communication skills – be honest and no waffling
- clarity about what you are offering
- fully addressing the clients' key requirements and fears
- presentations – keep them brief and to the point
- project portfolios – maintain them in good order and tailor them appropriately
- brochures, etc. – have something specific to leave behind which includes all contact details
- ensure it is a two-way interview – and listen to any responses
- impromptu sketching – can be effective, but only if you are good at it.

Negotiation

Securing work at any price is inevitably not good business for either side and you need the skills to negotiate good deals for your company while keeping your client happy. The negotiation will not only be about price, but will also include the nature and extent of the service, programme and delivery, quality and client expectations. Both sides may have established rules of engagement that need to be understood and reconciled. The aim is to ensure that both sides end up with a clear understanding of what they are to both provide and receive, whether it is services or fees, and that no surprises appear later on that might derail the relationship. This understanding needs to be expressed in writing, partly in the form of an appointment document (see Work Stage J) and partly as an exchange of letters or memoranda that spell out the terms of the deal.

See:
*Appointment,
page 105*

You need skill and skills to conduct the delicate dance of negotiation well. As with marketing ability and interview technique, getting professional training may prove to be an extremely valuable investment.

Generating your own work

The alternative to persuading others to hire you is to set up projects yourself. This usually involves finding and identifying sites and assessing the building opportunities, possibly talking to planning officers and discovering site owners. Good local knowledge helps with this, as does knowing where funding and grants might be accessed and who would be interested in taking on the risk of developing it.

Introducing a project to a developer or others who are keen to build (possibly including housing associations and certain private clients) should bring with it an introduction fee (to be negotiated) and the strong likelihood of being taken on as the architect. Some architects have become very good at this and can provide clients very rapidly with option appraisals, feasibility studies and development economics for projects. The ability to do effective appraisals requires a developer's understanding of how particular projects can create a profit or fit within available funding envelopes, even if it does not require the developer's willingness to take the financial risk.

If you are willing to carry that risk then you might choose to act as the developer yourself and take the project forward (although not necessarily through all the

Negotiation techniques

Negotiation is a vital skill for running a successful practice. The following techniques will give you confidence in your position and will help you to negotiate successfully:

Set objectives in advance:

- put your objectives in writing
- identify all the issues to be agreed
- establish your preferred outcome(s) and priorities
  - scope of services
  - your terms and conditions
  - design and quality standards
  - time required
  - principles to be adhered to
  - fees
  - warranties, etc.
- know where and how far you are prepared to compromise.

Understand the other side:

- know what is of importance to them
- know how keen they are to use you and therefore your relative bargaining power
- match their negotiating team with your own
- anticipate their offers with considered responses
- get your timing right.

Conduct:

- set the terms of the negotiation
- get points of agreement established
- clarify and record points of agreement as you proceed
- avoid negotiating in a climate of hostility – if necessary delay or postpone.

Continued

Tactics:

- recognise and anticipate common negotiating tricks designed to apply pressure, including:
  - the 'nibble' – adding additional requirements just after a deal is concluded
  - the 'flinch' – deliberately ridiculing an offer using body language
  - 'deferring to a higher authority' – apparently being unable to agree further
  - 'good cop, bad cop'
  - 'take it or leave it'
  - 'company policy says ...'
  - appeals to moral authority
  - splitting the difference
  - deadlines
- take a break if necessary
- avoid or use with caution similar pressure tactics
- do not accept the first offer
- if a lower price is offered, offer a lower level of service
- consider breaking the offer/price down element by element.

Know your own value:

- communicate it confidently
- be unemotional in weighing it against the offer from the other side
- be prepared to walk away.

Remember:

- use fairness and even-handedness as a measure
- both sides should emerge feeling happy and with honour satisfied
- you are going to have to work closely together so a good relationship is important
- a successful long-term relationship may be worth more that a short-term gain
- put a value on goodwill.

development stages before selling) using investment funding from banks and others. Many architects have found that this is a very effective way to design and build what they believe is the right solution, as well as usefully cutting out the developer and gaining (or potentially massively losing) the real profits to be made on a development project. Some architects do this in a more controlled way by developing and then selling their own homes or offices, while others have set up separate development companies and take a fully commercial approach.

It is beyond the scope of this guide to discuss development in any detail. It should not be attempted without appropriate knowledge, skill and advice, but having some of that skill and the ability to understand and find projects that will attract a developer's entrepreneurial spirit can be a great strength to an architectural practice and may keep it in work when other sources have run dry.

Saying 'No'

Architects tell many stories about the money and effort they would have saved if they had declined a commission from a prospective client at their first meeting. These situations are often clear at the time, but a combination of a desire to please, the challenge of the problem and a hunger for work frequently gets in the way of better judgement. Resist the temptation to do all and any work that crosses your path, and maintain your focus on what you set out to do.

When to think twice

- The budget is too small to contain the client's ambitions.
- There is not enough money available to pay for the project.
- Credit checks are less than satisfactory.
- The client is talking to large numbers of possible architects (and others).
- The client has already hired (and fired) other architects or has a reputation for litigation.
- The proposed fees are too small for you to properly resource the job.
- There is an expectation of considerable work prior to appointment (possibly in competition with others).
- Payment of fees is contingent on achieving planning consent.
- The programme for the work is too short or you cannot provide the necessary resources for the proposed timetable.
- The appointment is for only one or two stages at a time.
- The appointment requires skills that you do not possess or cannot obtain.
- The nature of the work conflicts with your principles, preferred style or working approach, etc.
- You will be expected to work or act in an unprofessional manner.
- You do not think that you will be able to work happily or satisfactorily with the client.
- You struggle to get payment on your first invoice.
- The risks attached to being involved outweigh the likely benefits.

CHECKLIST

Work Stage H: Winning work

☐ Ensure that you have the skills to convert a lead into a deal. Get training if necessary.

☐ Go into interviews practised, confident and well prepared.

☐ Know your value and how much you are prepared to give to win the job.

☐ Know how much you are prepared to work at risk for a particular job and client. Beware of being taken for a ride.

☐ Research your potential client and what matters to them.

☐ Make yourself familiar with negotiation techniques. Actively consider a training course. Understand the rules and apply them as unemotionally as possible.

☐ Match a lower offer with a lower level of service.

☐ Consider setting up and generating projects yourself.

☐ Always be prepared to say NO if the costs and risks outweigh the potential benefits.

Work Stage J
Appointments and fees

You have agreement in principle with a client that you will work for them, you now need to agree your terms of appointment and fees and get that agreement accurately set down on paper and signed by both parties.

Appointment

The RIBA publishes a number of different appointment documents to suit projects of different sizes and types. These documents range from the Standard Form of Agreement for the Appointment of an Architect (SFA/99) to the Small Works form (SW/99), with other forms for sub-consultants, interior design, project management, Planning Supervisor, etc. To accompany these forms there is also *A Client's Guide to Engaging an Architect* (RIBA, 2004). Further details are given in the book *The Architects Contract: Guide to RIBA Forms of Appointment* (RIBA Publishing, 2004). These forms, which are regularly updated to take account of changing legal and economic circumstances, are available in both print and online versions. They provide a useful basis for formalising an appointment, although there are alternative forms available, including the NEC Professional Services Contract and others.

The use of standard forms brings many advantages, including backup in the form of guidance and advice and the benefit of the experience of others. But you must still take great care to get the appointment right:

- Set down the scope of works accurately.
- Ensure the appointment interlocks with those of other consultants.
- Ensure the appointment is appropriate for the project and client.
- There must be clarity on what is to be expected and delivered by all parties.

In particular it is worth noting the impact of the Unfair Contract Terms in Consumer Contracts Regulations 1999, which in Regulation 5 states:

5(1) A contractual term which has not been individually negotiated shall be regarded as unfair if, contrary to the requirement of good faith, it causes a significant imbalance in the parties' rights and obligations arising under the contract, to the detriment of the consumer.

This requires that if the client is a residential occupier ('the consumer') then the terms of the appointment agreement should be individually negotiated with them to make them enforceable. How possible this is in practice is another matter, and it is worth following the advice from the RIBA and others on this to ensure that your agreement will have adequate force.

An appointment as a designer also brings with it responsibilities under the Construction (Design and Management) Regulations 1994 (CDM). The principal obligations are to identify at the design stage and eliminate or avoid risks to health and safety in construction work and to pass necessary information on risks to the appointed Planning Supervisor. In practice it is also frequently necessary to explain the requirement for, and then to arrange and ensure the appointment of, an appropriate Planning Supervisor by the client so that this can happen.

Note that the CDM Regulations are currently under revision and changes are due to be implemented in 2007 that will combine the CDM Regulations 1994 and the Construction (Health, Safety and Welfare) Regulations 1996 into a single regulatory package. Check with the Health and Safety Executive (www.hse.gov.uk) for further information.

However you seek to arrange matters, you need to ensure that an appointment, in writing, is in place for all projects that the practice undertakes, so that both Standard 11 of the ARB's *Architects Code: Standards of Conduct and Practice* and Guidance Note 4 of the *RIBA Code of Professional Conduct* are complied with.

Professional standards for appointments

ARB Standard 11

11.1   Architects should not undertake professional work unless the terms of the contract have been recorded in writing as to:

- the scope of the work;
- the fee or method of calculating it;
- the allocation of responsibilities;
- any limitation of responsibilities;
- the provisions for termination;
- any special provisions for dispute resolution;

and they have informed the client that Architects are subject to the disciplinary sanction of the Board in relation to complaints of unacceptable professional conduct or serious professional incompetence.

RIBA Code of Professional Conduct Guidance Note 4

4.1   Terms of Appointment
When proposing or confirming an appointment, a member should ensure that its terms and scope of works are clear and recorded in writing.

4.2   When contracting to supply architectural services, the terms of appointment should include:

- a clear statement of the client's requirements;
- a clear definition of the services required;
- the obligation to perform the services with due skill and care;
- the obligation to keep the client informed of progress;
- the roles of other parties who will provide services to the project;
- the name of any other person(s) with authority to act on behalf of the client;
- procedures for calculation and payment of fees and expenses;
- any limitation of liability and insurance;
- provisions for protection of copyright and confidential information;
- provisions for suspension and determination;
- provisions for dispute resolution.

Fees

Appointment documents will spell out the fees due at various stages of the project and for any particular tasks carried out, but first you need to agree the fees and a method for calculating them.

From your side, the fees you charge should:

- allow you to resource the job adequately
- cover additional non-fee earning overheads, such as premises costs, administration, insurance, recruitment, training, research and marketing
- pay for any specific, job-related expenses
- reward you for any risk taken
- reward you for the reputation, skill and track record of your business
- allow a reasonable level of profit
- be regular enough to ensure reasonable cash flow
- be predictable enough to allow you to plan ahead.

There may be good reason for discounting your fees in order to attract new clients or business, but such discounts will have to be balanced by additional fees charged elsewhere.

From the client's point of view, the fees should generally be less than:

- the added value provided by your services less any risk they carry in using your services
- the cost of obtaining an equivalent (or possibly simply adequate) service from other sources
- the amount that they have available to spend (balanced across the whole project)
- the amount they can provide at any one time from their cash flow.

Fees can be calculated in a variety of ways, based on:

- time
- a percentage of the contract cost
- a lump sum (or a series of lump sums)
- a share of any profits made or increase in value achieved
- a combination of the above.

The way fees are charged rarely directly reflects either your needs or those of your client. You need to calculate whether the fees to be paid will both cover your business requirements and sit within the client's spending envelope. You should ideally be able to demonstrate both of these, and therefore be able to maximise your fee within the client's available resources.

Payment schedule

The proportions of fees to be paid at each stage of a project, as specified in a payment schedule, has long been a matter of contention, particularly when the scope of works is subject to change. It is vital to get this right so that it will provide a reasonable cash flow to the practice to support the work on the project. The apportionment should be clearly laid out in the appointment document, and there should be provision for fees to be invoiced for on a monthly (or a more frequent) basis.

You should aim to weight the apportionment of fees at the front end of the job (in line with the hours expended on the project). The fees will have to cover numerous factors, including:

• the considerable costs involved in landing the job
• the up-front investment and resourcing required
• the risk of the job running into trouble or even being cancelled at planning, procurement or any other stage in the delivery process.

Your client may choose not to see it in the same light and it will be down to your negotiating skills to achieve a schedule acceptable to both sides.

The RIBA no longer publishes any recommended or indicative fee scales following developments in competition law, but fee guidance based on statistical data, including information on proportions charged for each project stage, is available from the RIBA (contact the Members' Information Line on 020 7307 3600).

Expenses

The appointment should be clear about the expenses that may be charged and any additional handling charge involved in addition to the fees. Typically, expenses will include travel, postage and printing, but they may also include the purchase and copying of documents, drawings and maps. If you pay statutory fees, such as for planning and building regulations, directly then a charge for these should also be made.

CHECKLIST

Work Stage J: Appointments and fees

☐ Agree your appointment and ensure it is set down in writing and signed by both parties.

☐ Terms in contracts with residential occupiers (consumers) need to be individually negotiated.

☐ Ensure that a Planning Supervisor is appointed under the CDM regulations when necessary.

☐ Ensure your contract of appointment complies with both the ARB Standard and the RIBA Code of Professional Conduct.

☐ Ensure that you can deliver the agreed services for the agreed fee and still make a profit.

☐ Agree a payment schedule that allows you to maintain a near positive cash flow on the project.

Work Stage K
Working

This work stage examines the issues you may face as you get down to work. It anticipates that you are fully able to design and deliver all the stages of the RIBA Plan of Work and focuses instead on the management of the office that will support and protect you while you do so.

Professionalism

As an architect – a professional – you have professional responsibilities. Your professional status is there to both require and help you to work to a generally high standard. But crucially it should also enable you to act for the wider good of society, including to the benefit of a local community, the environment or for broader social or economic ends. In addition, by acting in an accepted and recognised professional manner, you are partly protected from accusation and threat of legal action.

Although the immediate rules of professional behaviour are set down in the ARB's *The Architects Code: Standards of Conduct and Practice* and the *RIBA Code of Professional Conduct*, the generally understood character of professionalism across society is constantly in development. It has been greatly affected by developments in other areas, such as the cases of Dr Harold Shipman and Alderhey Hospital, as well as some recent court cases against built environment professionals. One result of this change is that it is now not enough to behave in a professional manner – it is also necessary to be able to show that you have behaved professionally. Another result is the pressure on companies to not just rely on their professional employees to act professionally but also to ensure that they perform as professional entities themselves and that as corporate bodies they act in accordance with codes of ethics, standards and conduct.

The Architects Code: Standards of Conduct and Practice (ARB)

The Architects Code consists of ten 'Standards', supported by an introduction and further explanatory subclauses.

Standards

1. Architects should at all times act with integrity and avoid any action or situations which are inconsistent with their professional obligations.
2. Architects should only undertake professional work for which they are able to provide adequate professional, financial and technical competence and resources.
3. Architects should only promote their professional services in a truthful and responsible manner.
4. Architects should carry out their professional work faithfully and conscientiously and with due regard to relevant technical and professional standards.
5. In carrying out or agreeing to carry out professional work, Architects should pay due regard to the interests of anyone who may reasonably be expected to use or enjoy the products of their own work.
6. Architects should maintain their professional service and competence in areas relevant to their professional work, and discharge the requirements of any engagement with commensurate knowledge and attention.
7. Architects should preserve the security of monies entrusted to their care in the course of their practice or business.
8. Architects should not undertake professional work without adequate and appropriate professional indemnity insurance cover.
9. Architects should ensure that their personal and professional finances are managed prudently.
10. Architects should promote the Standards set out in this Code.

For further details see www.arb.org.uk.

RIBA Code of Professional Conduct

The code comprises

- three principles of professional conduct
- professional values that support those principles
- guidance notes that explain how the principles can be upheld.

Principles

1. Integrity
   Members shall act with honesty and integrity at all times.
2. Competence
   In the performance of their work Members shall act competently, conscientiously and responsibly. Members must be able to provide the knowledge, the ability and the financial and technical resources appropriate for their work.
3. Relationships
   Members shall respect the relevant rights and interests of others.

For further details see www.architecture.com.

Both the ARB and the RIBA have disciplinary procedures to enforce their codes of conduct – for further information see their websites, or refer to the companion guide *Keeping Out of Trouble* by Owen Luder (RIBA Publishing, 2006). Such procedures are very time-consuming and potentially highly damaging to an architect's career and so should be avoided, if at all possible, by proper compliance with both the spirit and the letter of the individual codes.

It is also beneficial to take an interest in the development of professional issues and become involved in the activities of the many bodies, such as the RIBA, ARB, CABE, government, local authorities and others, who are engaged in ensuring that standards of conduct and practice reflect the challenges of working in an ever-changing world.

Organisation

In order to be able to run jobs so that you meet all the requirements of your clients, insurers and the law, while also complying with professional codes of conduct, you need to be well organised and to have an adequate level of management to ensure that projects run smoothly and are provided with sufficient resources.

There is plenty of management advice and a wide variety of tools available to help you with this, including the *RIBA Plan of Work*, the *Architect's Job Book* and innumerable other sources of information. The following sections flag up a number of issues that you may wish to plan for as you establish management procedures for your practice.

Project staffing

Ensure that a named senior person in the practice is responsible for each job that the office takes on. If that person is not an architect it may also be necessary to name an architect to take responsibility for work carried out under the heading of 'Architect's Services' or 'Services to be Performed by an Architect'.

The projected staff resources, time and programme that any job will require can be mapped out and a relatively straightforward set of interlocking matrices produced to show the allocation of staff time to projects and how individuals' time will be spread over the various projects and other activities in the office. If required this mapping can be more sophisticated and made to link with production schedules, timesheets, job costing and progress reporting. But, if it is to remain useful, it must be kept up to date to reflect the realities of delays, interruptions and overruns that affect all jobs.

Such matrices should allow you to ensure that enough of the time of appropriately skilled and trained staff can be provided for each job, and will help you not only to keep track of resources, but also to plan ahead.

Records

As each job gets underway a system of record keeping will start for it. Most offices have a system of codes, starting with a job number but also encompassing standard drawing references, filing references, etc. The reference system should be based on a standard office model and where appropriate on industry-wide approaches, such as the Common Arrangement of Work Sections (CAWS) and the Coordinated Project Information (CPI) procedures.

Similarly, a number of files will need to be opened to become permanent repositories for the history of each job. The number of these files will depend on a job's likely complexity. A single file may well be adequate for a simple domestic job, but on more complex projects separate files will typically be required for:

- the client(s) and their affairs
- planning, statutory undertakers and building control
- health and safety and the Planning Supervisor
- the separate consultants
- specification and schedules
- the tender procedure
- the contractor
- sub-contractors and suppliers
- minutes of meetings
- Architect's Instructions
- valuations and certificates
- programmes, delays, etc.
- schedules of information required, etc.
- drawing issue and received sheets
- drawings (including superseded versions).

As the job progresses some of these files may grow to require several volumes. Computer records should be organised in a similar fashion. Print out and file e-mails in the same way as other correspondence, together with any other relevant memos, notes and information from manufacturers, standards agencies, etc.

At the end of each project the records need to be ordered and decisions made about what is to be kept for the medium and long terms. It is essential to retain any records that might be needed if a dispute arises at a later date, but no more than that. Files should be kept for a minimum of six years from the date of completion for contracts signed under hand, and twelve years for those signed under seal.

See also: Dealing with information, page 53

Quality control

An overall project plan and record should be developed for each job. This should flow from the practice's overall quality control procedure and become the core text for the project. It is a live document that will be amended and updated as the project proceeds and should describe any particular requirements of the project and how these will be achieved. The project quality plan (PQP) is a core element in the RIBA QM Toolkit, downloadable free to members from www.architecture.com, and its use is a minimum requirement to qualify for the RIBA Chartered Practice Scheme.

See also: Quality management, page 127–130

Project plan – typical contents

- Description
  - client(s)
  - site and constraints
  - brief and client requirements
  - life cycle
- Internal organisation
  - named responsible practice members and staff allocated to project
  - consultation and communication procedures
  - programme and timetables
- Project team
  - team members (client representatives, consultants, contractors, suppliers, etc.)
  - matrix of responsibilities
  - administration, communication and coordination procedures
- Project development
  - document control and administration
  - review procedures
  - development of brief
  - health and safety
  - design input and output
  - specification
  - procurement and tender process
  - contract administration
  - quality monitoring
  - valuation
- Change management
  - procedures
  - records
- Audit
  - inspections and tests
  - documentation
  - procedures for corrective action
  - post-occupancy evaluation
- Post-contract
  - inspection
  - project reviews and feedback
  - maintenance manuals and as-built information
  - project records

Change control

All projects develop and change as they progress through the office, with many of those involved requiring, recommending or making alterations and adjustments to both the brief and the outcomes as the work proceeds. Keeping up to date with these changes, understanding their implications and communicating this to all the parties involved is an important element in the effective handling of projects. Some practices recommend the use of change-control forms or other forms of record keeping to document each and every change on a project, with a collated version being distributed to the client and to the design and construction teams on a regular (monthly) basis. Such information, useful in itself to help the smooth running of projects, can also assist in explaining delays and with claims for additional fees.

Standard procedures

In order to maintain consistent levels of achievement on a repeat basis, you may wish to develop similar standard methodologies and solutions that can be regularly improved and transferred from project to project. Some standard procedures may be as simple as template forms for schedules or standard phrasing and descriptions; others may be more complex such as a library of standard details or a library of practice-specific specification clauses.

Standardising your outputs will be more costly and time-consuming at the beginning, at just the time when both money and time may be in short supply, but it should pay back richly later as they build up into an essential resource for effective practice.

Resourcing

Every project will have both intense and quiet times, and the workload will vary considerably over its life. This can put enormous stress on any practice's ability to cope. With luck a diverse set of projects in the office will permit some balance between projects, but it is just as likely to create simultaneous peaks of activity. Consider strategies for dealing with both busy times and quiet times that do not make excessive demands on staff or on everyone's family and home life.

Resourcing strategies

Potential strategies for managing resources include:

- maintaining a relationship with other practices to share staff time
- using freelance and temporary staff, preferably regulars who understand your working methods
- recruiting at times of need, and possibly maintaining growth to avoid subsequent redundancy
- outsourcing intensive work, such as detail drawing programmes, to external, and possibly overseas, suppliers
- only accepting work that you can fit into your current staffing schedule and working at your own speed
- balancing training and research activity with fee-earning work
- ensuring that there are projects in the office which are less time-dependent that can be turned to when the workload is slow
- using competitions and speculative work to act as a 'float', with the willingness to drop or postpone such work if schedules so dictate
- agreeing flexible working practices with staff
- carefully managing staff leave and holidays.

Time management

Part of the job of controlling and managing the resources of the business is ensuring that time is spent usefully. This does not mean that everyone should be constantly and furiously busy, but that time is allocated in a sensible and effective manner that allows work to be done, deadlines met and emergencies handled without resorting to last minute rushes, late night working and general panic.

There are some basic, and probably very familiar, tools that help with managing time:

- The diary – the office diary, with everyone's activities (both regular and one-off) marked in it, is an essential item of any office. Computerised diaries and calendars can help deal with the complexity generated by even a modest number of staff by giving both multiple and remote access to users.
- Timesheets – already discussed in Work Stage E and very valuable for assessing effectiveness against time spent. Detailed time logs carried out for short

periods of time (e.g. two weeks) and filled out continuously for every five- or ten-minute slot can also be very revealing of how time is really spent and may help with working out how to use it more productively.

- To do lists – a straightforward but very useful device to remind yourself and others what needs to be done. Tasks on the list should be given priority ratings and allocated both an amount of time and a target completion date or time. If individual tasks are large and unwieldy they should be broken down into smaller achievable tasks, each with their own priorities and timings.
- Work schedules – a plan for both short-term (daily) and medium-term (weekly or monthly) activities that allows activities to be mapped out. Comparison with to do lists will flag up whether it is possible to complete the allocated tasks within the time allowed.
- Delegating – while it is always tempting to do all and everything yourself, effective time management suggests that delegating, and possibly out-sourcing, activities is often far more effective and should allow you more time for doing what you are best at.

In architectural practice, just as in politics, events will do their best to derail your plans – it can be very easy to be led by them and the pressing need to respond to the latest issue or crisis. Usually there is more important work to be done, but as it is not so urgent it is tempting to put it to one side. Take the rational view – if necessary, tell today's siren voices to wait until the following day, when the crisis will usually have blown over. Set your own priorities and stick by them, you will only be respected for your calmness in the face of hostile fire.

Research and innovation

If your practice is to stay ahead of the competition it has to offer a continuously improving service and product. A 'continuous improvement' attitude requires, in turn, both research – including analysing feedback from clients and previous projects and innovation – and putting that research into action. Constructing Excellence (www.constructingexcellence.org.uk) provides key performance indicator (KPI) questionnaires that can be used to measure your performance against client expectations at key stages during the life of a project. The results can then be benchmarked against those from other similar firms. Being able to point to good user satisfaction levels can also become a powerful marketing tool for the firm.

See also:
Benchmarking,
page 126

Each project will have both a research and an innovation agenda, possibly including:

- briefing
- design issues
- products and materials
- specification
- procurement
- construction.

The knowledge gained from each project should be captured and recorded for re-use on future jobs. Much of the research activity for both current and future jobs can be included in required continuous professional development (CPD) programmes.

Risk

Every project carries risk – some would say that architects accept excessive amounts of risk with every commission they take on. Risk should be managed as proactively as possible in order that it is anticipated, understood, minimised and avoided. Make sure that someone is in charge of assessing and reducing the risk on each job, or maintain a risk register for each job recording the possible severity and likelihood of each risk identified and the avoidance and management actions to be taken. You are required to do this for the health and safety risks involved in constructing and maintaining your designs – do it for yourself as well, but make sure it does not turn into just another box-ticking exercise.

Ensure clients, contractors and others are formally and fully informed of any risks they carry and any actions that might be taken to avoid them.

Locums

If you run a single-handed practice or if all responsible staff are away simultaneously, you need to have in place a locum to cover for you during your absence or if you fall sick. The RIBA publishes a standard letter of agreement for locum appointments, available from the members-only area of its website.

Money

Each job has its own financial dynamic from the moment the appointment is agreed. This needs to be closely managed to ensure that:

- the job produces the anticipated income
- any additional works are recorded and invoiced for
- the allocated budget is not overspent without being acknowledged and the necessary action taken.

Invoicing should ideally be regular, and at least monthly, although some practices only charge at the completion of work stages or when other project milestones are attained. It is always better, if possible, to be paid in advance rather than after work has been carried out. Alternatively, fees and other monies can be deposited in a client account for withdrawal as agreed. If there is any doubt about a client's willingness or ability to pay fees, ensure that one of these two latter methods is employed. Consider issuing clients with a programme of likely payments to be made on a job – for you, other consultants and the contractor – so that they are forewarned and are able to plan their finances in advance.

Job costs and disbursements should be charged at regular intervals along with fees. Some practices charge a percentage fee to cover the normal range of job costs while others itemise and charge at cost or with the addition of a handling fee. Remember that paying out money for items in advance almost always has a higher cost than the stated face value, due to bank interest, charges for cheques, etc. If you buy goods for use by the client or for the works, you face increased risk if they are in any way faulty or need to be returned. If, for example, you supply an electrical fitting that malfunctions and causes a fire, it could be very expensive indeed.

Getting invoices paid promptly is an essential part of business practice. File invoices separately from the rest of the project paperwork and keep your records so that you are aware immediately if invoices become overdue. Maintain a robust system on outstanding invoices that includes reminder letters, faxes and e-mails, personal telephone calls and, if necessary, solicitor's letters and legal action. Some clients are inevitably better than others when it comes to paying bills promptly and it may be necessary to take their payment history into account before bearing down on them with the full force of the law.

Should it be necessary, you can make a claim yourself through a county court (see www.hmcourts-service.gov.uk) or online via the Courts Service (www.money claim.gov.uk). If the amount claimed is less than £5000 and the matter is relatively straightforward (e.g. not many witnesses need to be called) then it can be processed on the 'small claims track' and you should not require the services of a solicitor. This can make claiming both worthwhile and cost-effective and is a good argument for keeping invoices small and frequent.

Trouble

There is a companion volume in this series of RIBA Good Practice Guides called *Keeping Out of Trouble* (2006) which covers both avoiding problems and knowing what to do when they appear. There is also plenty of advice available in professional journals and from insurers.

Should you suspect that a problem has occurred or is likely to arise, take immediate action. Leaving it to sort itself out is immensely risky and the chances are that it will not, and may instead escalate. Seek advice from an appropriate party. If there is any possibility that the problem could result in a claim on your insurance policy, always notify your insurers immediately so that they can help you deal with the problem.

Taking on staff

The RIBA Good Practice Guide *Employment* deals with the legal aspects of employing staff and the workplace – these issues are not dealt with further here.

But as has already been noted, expanding a firm beyond the sole practitioner or original partners marks a gear shift in the nature and responsibility of the firm that requires a different approach to management. Employees have a number of needs that you will be responsible for providing, including:

- a decent workplace
- a worthwhile income and other benefits
- an interesting and regular stream of work
- information and communication
- motivation and leadership
- a positive and sociable working environment
- team building
- training and learning
- equipment
- reasonable and flexible hours
- holidays and leave
- job security

- equal opportunities and fairness
- career advancement
- respect, recognition and praise.

Plan to be able to respond positively to these requirements and manage the practice so that it can try to fulfil them.

CHECKLIST

Work Stage K: Working

- ☐ Understand your professional duties, and work (and be seen to work) in strict accordance with them.
- ☐ Plan your resources to match your commitments.
- ☐ Keep up-to-date and appropriate records for every job.
- ☐ Develop a project plan for every job. Use it to maintain standards and consistency as well as to deal with requirements that are special and particular to the project.
- ☐ Use each job to develop and improve standard procedures and knowledge.
- ☐ Manage risk rather than allowing it to run out of control.
- ☐ Keep a close watch over money, costs and cash flow on each project.
- ☐ Inform your insurers the moment you smell trouble.
- ☐ Treat your staff better than you treat yourself.

Work Stage L
Keeping going

Once your start-up business has turned into a more established presence different pressures will affect the way you work and the way you use your resources. You will need to know where you stand with respect to both your market and your competitors and ensure you stay ahead of both. A steady stream of work to maintain the practice will become more important as will the need to protect the investment that you have all made in building up the practice to this point.

Maturing

As your new practice emerges from the early, sometimes painful, set-up stage and begins to consolidate its position in the market, you will gradually need to take a different approach to running the business. Habits, good and bad, will have taken root, commitments will have been made and a track record will have built you a reputation among clients and others. You may still view the practice as young, up-and-coming and thrusting, and that view may stay with you for ever, but you also need to build on the work that has been achieved and to break free of any early typecasting that may be restricting your growth.

The problems of running an established business are different from those involved in setting one up. Keeping a steady workflow and ensuring that the monthly billing target is achieved become matters of much greater importance. There is greater complexity, with jobs now at very different stages and needing varying degrees of attention, and so more management effort is required, and you will have new competitors coming up on the inside track.

No one wants the practice to become stuck in its ways. It needs to maintain the vigour of its earliest period, to stay up to date and be able to reinvent itself, as and when necessary, to improve its competitiveness for both clients and staff. At the same time, the appetite for the long hours and late nights may have dimmed, and you will want and need to achieve a better work–life balance.

Benchmarking

Find out how you measure up as a practice in comparison with other businesses – your peers and competition. Benchmarking has now become a standard business tool to help companies assess their performance against a series of measures and to compare the results with other anonymous firms, both in their business sector or more widely. It can be used as a DIY tool, using your own chosen criteria, or as a formal process that will provide standardised results.

See the Benchmark Index (www.benchmarkindex.com), the BSI (www.bsi-emea. com/BenchMark) or the CBI (www.cbi.org.uk) for more information on bench-marking services. The RIBA provides an on-line benchmarking service as part of its Chartered Practice Scheme (www.architecture.com) and a bespoke bench-marking service, aimed specifically at architectural practices, is available from Colander together with *The Architects' Journal* (www.colander.co.uk).

Benchmarking

Benchmark assessment topics can include:

- company structure
- resources, including capital
- profits and turnover
- costs
- conversion rate of leads into fee-paying work
- number, types and sizes of live projects
- percentage of repeat work
- fees and rates charged
- staff numbers, seniority levels and qualifications
- salaries and benefits
- employment terms
- gender, age and ethnic origin ratios
- staff satisfaction
- premises: areas, types and costs
- IT systems
- quality assurance systems
- corporate social responsibility (CSR)
- training
- marketing
- research and development
- customer perception and satisfaction.

Reviewing

Periodically and regularly review the development of the practice, allowing for specific time-outs with partners or directors and discussions with staff, clients, advisers and fellow consultants. Check against the original vision and practice objectives and take corrective action as necessary.

Knowledge management

Take stock of what you and the practice know. This guide has emphasised the desirability of capturing your knowledge as it is learnt and developed. Consider whether you are using this knowledge to best effect and how it might serve you better. If appropriate, formalise and develop the office procedures into a more effective tool, possibly in the form of an office manual or a quality management system (QMS).

An office manual should be as comprehensive and up to date as is reasonable, as well as being easy to navigate and accessible for a newcomer to the practice. The manual should give a clear understanding of the practice approach and means of dealing with a wide range of situations. The QMS will amplify this and provide greater detail and depth. A single person in the office should have responsibility for both the manual and the QMS. (See overleaf for possible outline contents of an office manual.)

Quality management

You may want to take this process further and achieve a recognised quality management system standard. The best known of these standards is the ISO (International Standards Organization) 9000 series, which includes ISO 9001 certification, administered by the British Standards Institute (see www.bsi-global. com). Also known as quality accreditation (QA), such standards are intended to help you to:

- achieve greater consistency
- reduce mistakes
- increase efficiency
- improve customer satisfaction
- market your business more effectively and in new sectors and areas
- manage growth more effectively
- continually improve your products and services.

Office manual

The outline contents of an office manual might include:

1. The practice
    ○ organisation and structure
    ○ practice vision and objectives
    ○ policy statements
    ○ lines of responsibility
2. Office management
    ○ quality management system
    ○ health and safety
    ○ IT and communications
    ○ knowledge and information management
    ○ standard documentation
    ○ filing and record keeping
    ○ archiving
    ○ accounting procedures
    ○ equipment and materials
    ○ PR, promotion and marketing
    ○ transport policy
3. Staff
    ○ equal opportunities and employment policy
    ○ health and safety and work conditions
    ○ general terms of engagement
    ○ working hours and overtime
    ○ leave entitlement and procedure
    ○ qualifications/registration/memberships
    ○ code of behaviour
    ○ complaints procedure
    ○ discipline procedure
4. Training and research
    ○ aims and objectives
    ○ CPD

Continued

    ○ student employment

    ○ papers and publications

5. Incoming projects

    ○ speculative work and competitions

    ○ appointment procedure and sign-off

    ○ internal team selection

    ○ external team appointments

6. Design management

    ○ aims and objectives

    ○ design procedures

    ○ quality control procedures

    ○ detail design and production information

    ○ specification preparation

    ○ design change procedures

    ○ health and safety

7. Job administration

    ○ health and safety

    ○ information collection

    ○ compliance checking

    ○ permissions and approvals

    ○ cost and programme controls

    ○ resource management

    ○ reporting procedures

    ○ contract correspondence

    ○ instructions and certificates

    ○ record keeping

    ○ meetings

    ○ site visits

8. General procedures

    ○ risk register and risk management

    ○ corrective and preventative actions

    ○ emergency procedures

    ○ audit and feedback

Accreditation may not necessarily improve the quality of your product or the service you give to your clients. However, you may find that many clients, especially those from the public sector, will require their suppliers and consultants to have ISO 9001 certification and so you might lose business and business opportunities if you do not obtain it.

The RIBA provides a free Quality Management Toolkit that accords with ISO 9001, and is downloadable from the members-only area of its website (www.architecture.com). The toolkit includes further information on the standard and how to achieve it. If you do intend to seek certification you are well advised to seek assistance from an external specialist consultant in order to develop your quality management system fully in advance. Achieving certification requires assessment and approval from a recognised accredited certification body, payment of fees for certification assessments, occasional surveillance visits thereafter and annual registration. It does not come cheap, but it may prove necessary and possibly very worthwhile.

Workload

After several years of practice the workload should have matured too. Ideally, you will have fewer small awkward projects that struggle to be profitable and a greater proportion of larger and possibly more challenging jobs. You may have successfully obtained a regular flow of work from mainstream clients and such work will have brought with it more established staffing and resourcing patterns.

Assess your workload to see if it is providing:

- a range of different projects to balance cross-sectoral risk
- a range of clients and types of clients, with no more than 25 per cent of fee income from a single source
- projects at different work stages
- bread-and-butter work, coming in at a regular pace
- higher profile projects that can help promote the practice
- commissions that can help the practice develop and maintain specialisms or expertise in key areas
- work from growth sectors of the economy
- a match between staffing levels and workload
- work to enthuse and retain yourself and your staff
- new clients and new building types.

With more of a track record and greater experience, marketing the practice and bringing in work should become more straightforward – but you may also find that more depends on you maintaining that workflow. There will be a constant need for a stream of new work to replace that currently underway in the office, and as the moment requiring the greatest effort to achieve this will be when the practice is at its busiest, there may never be any time to let up.

Skills

As the workload shifts so will the need to ensure that the practice maintains the right skills to attract new work and to carry it out. New skills will be required, following changes in the market, developments in ideas, products and technology and simply as part of keeping up to date. Some of these skills can be developed among existing staff as part of training and CPD, others may require recruitment of new personnel.

The practice will need to keep track of the range of skills it requires and can develop or afford. Action will be required to maintain and achieve the right mixture and level of skills, experience and enthusiasm if the practice is to stay on top of its game.

The practice may also wish to take on students as part of the staff mix. This will involve commitment to provide training and experience as well as work and pay. In turn the practice may gain considerably from the recent training, curiosity and freshness that a student can bring. The RIBA has published guidance on employing students, including model contracts, which is available from its Professional Education and Development Resource website (www.pedr.co.uk).

Planning for disaster

Disaster may strike in many ways. Some disasters may be so extreme that recovery from them will only be worked out at the time. However, many potentially catastrophic events happen on a regular basis to all sorts of businesses and are largely predictable – such events can and should be planned for, as well as insured against.

• Natural disasters – including floods, burst water pipes (due to cold weather), storm damage, etc. The likelihoods will vary depending on your location. Consider measures that can prevent avoidable damage and can allow you to carry on elsewhere almost immediately should it happen.

- Theft – especially of equipment and, potentially, of stored information. Ensure that office premises are secure – install security devices and alarms as necessary. Maintain a register of all your equipment, recording serial numbers and values. Follow up with regular checks and audits. Allocate responsibility for items of equipment to individuals. Lock equipment to furniture or the building fabric. Permanently mark or electronically tag equipment. Regularly or automatically back up information and store it securely, away from the main site.
- Vandalism – both physical vandalism and computer viruses, etc. can disable your business. Take precautionary measures to protect staff, premises and equipment.
- Fire and explosion – can be devastating for a business, but loss of information can be far worse than the loss of premises or equipment.
- Illness or incapacity of key staff – can strike at any time. How might you cope? Is all relevant information recorded in a clear manner to allow work to be picked up by other members of staff? Are you insured?
- Legal action or a formal complaint – whether from clients, contractors or others, and whether reasonable or not, may need to be defended. How would you find the time, energy, costs and relevant advice to deal with such a threat?
- Damage to reputation – How would you respond to negative press stories or scares? Would you know whom you could turn to to manage the issue?

Work–life balance

However it may seem at the time, there is a life beyond architecture and the making of buildings. Around any company there is a wider community of people – friends, relatives and dependants – who need attention as much as the people in the office. Ensure they are all treated with consideration and imagination.

Allow for adequate holidays and time off for sickness or for family matters, and allow the greater richness of the world beyond the office to fully inform the way you run your practice.

CHECKLIST

Work Stage L: Keeping going

☐ Benchmark your practice against other businesses and competitors.

☐ Ensure you carry out regular reviews of the development, standing and prospects of the business.

☐ Develop a comprehensive office manual.

☐ Put in place a quality management system and consider achieving ISO 9001 certification.

☐ Review the practice's workload to ensure that it is delivering the optimum mix of quality and quantity of work.

☐ Maintain and extend the skills and experience base in the office.

☐ Plan for disaster – do not be wise only after the event.

☐ Ensure you maintain a good work–life balance – have a life beyond work.

Work Stage M
Evaluation and looking ahead

All businesses periodically need to take stock and to renew themselves. Do this methodically and prepare a new business plan just as you prepared the first, but with a wealth of experience on which to base it. Make sure you consider and plan for the future. This may include both targeting new sectors of work and making changes in personnel, including those at the top.

The (next) business plan

After an immense amount of work you have an established and smooth running practice that is a credit to your business and professional abilities. It is now time to revisit the whole process. You started by preparing a business plan – this should now be reviewed and the actual outcomes evaluated against the original vision. How was the performance? Were the objectives achieved? How will this inform the follow-up plan?

The SWOT analysis must be repeated – as it should already have been in the interim – and the process of establishing a new business plan begun. Several years into the practice's life there should now be many more people – clients, planners, staff, users, etc. – whose opinions can be garnered, whether good, bad or indifferent. If possible, get an outside neutral person or body to carry out this study for you, and be prepared to face up to (and possibly share) and act on the results. Do not forget to take your own views into account.

Note: Specific key performance indicators (KPIs) for 'client satisfaction – service' are available from Constructing Excellence – see www.kpizone.com.

The new business plan should take the results of your analysis into account, but it does not have to prostrate itself before them. You may wish to sharpen any new business objectives considerably and, for example, use the achievement of specific user satisfaction levels as a target to be reached within a defined time period. Developing a new plan may, in one way, be more difficult – it can be hard to plot a new direction when you also need to keep the business going day to day – but you will also come to it knowing what actions can be effective and where to concentrate your energy.

Remember that the best time to set off in a new direction will be when you are at your most successful. It is extremely difficult to manage this sort of change when the business is in the middle of a downturn or decline.

Forward planning

Planning, even for the relatively short term of a business plan, requires looking into the future and making predictions. If possible, approach this in a spirit of serious enquiry, and use one or more of the formal techniques available (see box). Alternatively, gain access to others' research and analysis into prospects for the sectors you are most interested in. There are several consultancies that provide this as a commercial service or can carry out tailored studies on your behalf.

The results will be far from foolproof – future gazing does not provide a great degree of certainty – but both they and the process of reaching them can help you to focus on issues that are not of immediate concern but may become so in the years ahead.

Architecture has a tendency to be a responsive profession – waiting for clients with building needs to come to it. The business of architecture, on the other hand, is likely to become increasingly entrepreneurial, and it is those who are willing to look forward and take informed risks who are most likely to succeed.

Practice positioning

Looking into the future, if nothing else, should have helped to suggest where you see the practice being within five to ten years' time and how you want it to be perceived by clients, various communities of interest, your peers, etc. Backcasting in particular can suggest ways in which the practice could reposition itself and achieve a more positive and deliberate role and business outlook.

Getting to where you want to be should form an essential part of your new business plan, but it may take considerable commitment to establish a fresh or reworked identity. Fees may fall off as the practice repositions itself and focuses on winning new areas of business on its own terms. It is likely to require a degree

Looking into the future

The following methodologies can be applied to forward planning:

- **Projecting** (Quantitative trend analysis) – uses past experience and data to extrapolate forward. Can be relatively accurate if you have good figures and the environment is relatively stable. Not good in periods of change. A starting point for discussion.
- **Trend spotting** (Qualitative trend analysis) – typically based on the observations of workshop participants in response to open questions. Good at spotting change and risk. Weak at differentiating between short- and long-term trends.
- **Predicting** (Delphi survey) – uses the input of panels of 'experts' or knowledgeable stakeholders working together to build a consensus view. More accurate than the view of a single 'expert', but may tend towards the pessimistic. Combine with other methods.
- **Scenario building** – the development of alternative futures for testing by panels of experts, users, etc. Will not predict the future but may indicate areas of potential stability and change. A powerful tool, but one that depends on the quality of the scenarios. Useful for generating debate.
- **Backcasting** – the construction of narratives exploring how a predicted or intended future was achieved by looking back from a future vantage point. Can be part of the scenario method. Best at planning for predetermined outcomes.
- **Wild cards** – the use of radical propositions or extreme events to aid brainstorming and get debate flowing. May serve as early warning device but is very dependent on the quality of the participants.
- **Future workshops** – visioning and brainstorming workshops – often used to gather a wide range of ideas and opinions. Can be good for large-scale participation but can become unduly downbeat.

See *A Futurist's Toolbox* (Performance and Innovation Unit, The Cabinet Office, 2001).

of reskilling and retraining of partners/directors and staff so that they are able to work in a different sector or take a new approach.

Size and growth

See: Size and growth, page 36

The issue of how big a practice you want to run was raised in Work Stage D, during the previous discussion on the business plan. As you evaluate the progress of the practice you will inevitably review this.

Many firms chose to stay at a size that they have discovered, possibly through trial and error, suits them, while others will grow and shrink to adapt to match the workload that they have at any one time. Growth can clearly bring many benefits, including a wider diversity of projects, but in an architecture practice, as with any other business, it brings its own problems and needs to be planned for. Structures and management styles that suited a smaller outfit may no longer work so well – staffing hierarchies may have to be established and new premises found. The economics of growth can be a hard mistress and frequently drive a quest for further growth. The prospect of downsizing again in the event of a recession can also be daunting.

Some projects are now only available to practices over a certain size, either because clients are looking for a degree of reassurance that size brings or because the pace and response times are such that only larger practices can provide the almost instant ability to allocate staff to projects while bearing the risk that the project might never materialise. In addition, the size of practice that is 'big enough' to achieve this appears to be growing all the time and may always stay, elusively, beyond reach.

Staff progression

If you have staff, they will have career ambitions. This may lead to them moving on to gain experience elsewhere or to set up their own firm, possibly in competition with yours. This can mean the loss of considerable expertise and knowledge as well as the fracturing of a well-established team. At its worst they could also take clients and work away with them. At its best it might be a long-awaited relief and provide openings for others in the firm.

Providing opportunities for advancement for talented staff can be a serious problem for practices and it often produces pressure for growth and expansion

Planning for growth/change

As part of your future planning, you should consider the following issues:

- Review of current performance
  - benchmarking
  - risk and risk management
  - best practice
- The vision for growth
  - objectives
  - options
  - expansion vs. acquisition or merger
  - alternatives (e.g. consortia, joint ventures, partnering)
  - (re)branding
- The business plan
  - opportunity areas or sectors
  - knowledge and skills
  - available resources
  - innovation and specialisms
  - changing business structure
  - working methods
  - business targets
  - marketing
  - current client base
  - outsourcing
  - quality management procedures
  - infrastructure
  - premises
  - satellite offices
- Finance
  - raising finance
  - equity and shareholders
- Personnel
  - management team
  - roles and promotions
  - performance and incentives
  - reorganising or restructuring
- Advisers
  - choice of advisers

as well as a shift from a partnership to a company structure. Various ways can be used to recognise and encourage staff, including titles such as 'associate' or financial reward schemes, but these may be insufficient to prevent them moving on. Ensure this issue is openly discussed and strategies developed to deal with it if necessary.

Succession planning

A more advanced aspect of the staff progression problem is planning for the succession of the firm as partners and directors decide to retire or step into another role. This may involve passing the leadership baton to more junior members of the practice – with an agreement as to how the capital invested and built up might be released – or possibly even selling the firm to an external bidder. Inevitably, it is a process fraught with problems – the possibility of bruised egos and disintegration of the very asset that is being transferred due to the loss of key staff being among them. Take advice, address it over the long term and possibly restructure the firm with an eventual succession in mind long before it becomes inevitable.

CHECKLIST

Work Stage M: Evaluation and looking ahead

☐ Start work on your next business plan. The best time for this is when the business is at its most successful and running efficiently and smoothly.

☐ Repeat the process of evaluation and SWOT analysis from your first business plan.

☐ Take time and space to look at the future.

☐ Consider becoming more entrepreneurial and taking calculated risks.

☐ Formulate a plan to position the practice where you want it to be before the end of the next business planning cycle.

☐ Plan for the career advancement of your staff and your own succession.

Starting a practice
Conclusion

The essential question, raised at the start of this guide, remains: Why would you want to start a practice? The hours are long and the rewards paltry. The lifestyle can be enjoyable and the achievements, for all their relative size, very satisfying – but would they be enough if you were still working for that big outfit where you started your career?

CHECKLIST

A final summary checklist

Commitment

☐ Do you know why you want to start a new practice?
☐ Do you know what it involves?
☐ Are you prepared to stick with it?
☐ Can you cope with uncertainty and risk? Can your family or partner?
☐ How thick is your skin?

The business plan

☐ What is your business idea?
☐ Is there a gap in the market?
☐ Have you done your research?
☐ Who is the competition?
☐ What are your skills?
☐ Where are you getting your advice?
☐ Where will you be located?
☐ Who will buy your service?
☐ How will you market and promote the firm?

CONTINUED ▶

CHECKLIST CONTINUED ▶

☐ How will you finance the business?
☐ Will it make a profit?

The practice

☐ Do you have the necessary management skills?
☐ Can you read a page of accounts?
☐ Do you need further training?
☐ How big do you want the firm to be?
☐ Do you need staff?

Marketing

☐ Are you prepared to go out and sell the practice?
☐ Do you have a good sales pitch?
☐ Do you know how clients think?
☐ Do you know how to set up a website?
☐ Do you have a good address book?

Your role

Are you:

☐ a designer?
☐ a business leader?
☐ a professional?
☐ a manager?
☐ all of the above?

If you are going to do it, then doing it well and effectively is essential. It is still true that, despite the prominence of very big companies, most of the really good and exciting work is done by practices and firms that started small and can still remember what it was like. If you are absolutely sure that starting up a new practice is what you want to do, then good luck and good designing.

Bibliography and websites

Bibliography

Good Practice Guide Series, RIBA Publishing

Keeping Out of Trouble, Owen Luder, 3rd edition (2006)
Negotiating the Planning Maze, John Collins and Philip Moren (2006)
Employment, Brian Gegg and David Sharp (2006)

Other publications

The Architect's Plan of Work, Roland Phillips (ed.), RIBA Publications (2000)
Architect's Handbook of Practice Management, Sarah Lupton (ed.), RIBA Publications, 7th edition (2001)
Architect's Job Book, Sarah Lupton (ed.), RIBA Enterprises, 7th edition (2002)
An Architect's Guide to Running a Practice, David Littlefield, Architectural Press (2005)
The Architect in Practice, David Chappell and Christopher J. Willis, Blackwell Scientific, 8th edition (2000)
Start Up and Run Your Own Business: all you need to make it work, Jonathan Reuvid, Kogan Page Limited, 3rd edition (2004)
The No-Nonsense Guide to Government Rules and Regulations for Setting up Your Own Business, Business Link, DTI (2006)
Starting and Running Your Own Business, Barclays (2005)
The Architects Contract: Guide to RIBA Forms of Appointment, RIBA Publishing (2004)
Introduction to EU Procurement Rules, Office of Government Commerce (2006)
A Futurist's Toolbox, Performance and Innovation Unit, The Cabinet Office (2001)

The office library

Code of Professional Conduct, RIBA (2005)
Architects Code: Standards of Conduct and Practice, ARB

Planning Policy Statements (PPSs) and Planning Policy Guidance Notes (PPGs), The Stationery Office (TSO) (various dates)

The Building Regulations 2000 – Approved Documents, NBS

BSI Catalogue, BSI

Good Building Guides, Good Repair Guides, Information Papers and *Digests*, BRE

Standard Letters in Architectural Practice, David Chappell, Blackwell Publishing, 3rd edition (2003)

Metric Handbook: planning and design data, David Adler, Heinemann-Butterworth, 2nd edition (1999)

Neufert Architects Data, Ernst Neufert and Peter Neufert, Blackwell Science, 3rd edition (2002)

Architects Working Details, volumes 1–10, BRE/CRC (2005)

Robust Details Part E, Robust Details (2004)

Places, Streets and Movement, Alan Baxter & Associates, DETR (1998)

Urban Design Compendium, English Partnerships and the Housing Corporation (2000)

By Design, CABE, Thomas Telford (2000)

Building Bulletins, DfES, TSO (various dates)

BCO Guide 2005 – Best Practice in the Specification of Offices, British Council for Offices (BCO) (2005)

Forms of Appointment for an Architect, RIBA

A Clients Guide to Engaging an Architect, RIBA Publishing (2004)

JCT 05 Forms of Contract, Sweet and Maxwell (2005)

NBS Building, NBS

RIBA Product Selector, RIBA Enterprises

Barbour Index, CMPi

Websites

General

RIBA	www.architecture.com
RIAS	www.rias.org.uk
Business Link	www.businesslink.gov.uk
Small Business Service (part of DTI)	www.sbs.gov.uk
Smallbusiness.co.uk	www.smallbusiness.co.uk
Architects Registration Board	www.arb.org.uk

Banks – all tend to offer start-up advice

NatWest	www.natwest.com/business
Barclays	www.business.barclays.co.uk
Lloyds TSB	www.lloydstsbbusiness.com
HSBC	www.hsbc.co.uk/business
Co-op	www.co-operativebank.co.uk

Business information

Belbin Associates	www.belbin.com
Team Technology	www.teamtechnology.co.uk
Building magazine	www.building.co.uk
Mirza & Nacey	www.mirza-nacey.com
Architectyourhome	www.architect-yourhome.com

Company structure and naming

Companies House	www.companieshouse.gov.uk
Nominet	www.nic.uk

Tax

HM Revenue and Customs	www.hmrc.gov.uk

Data protection

Information Commissioner's Office	www.ico.gov.uk

Health and safety

Health and Safety Executive (HSE)	www.hse.gov.uk
Construction Skills Certification Scheme	www.cscs.uk.com
Construction Industry Training Board (CITB)	www.citb-constructionskills.co.uk
Construction Industry Council	www.cic.org.uk

Insurance

RIBA Insurance Agency	www.architectspi.com

Pensions

The Pensions Regulator	www.pensionsregulator.gov.uk

Procurement

Construction Line	www.constructionline.co.uk
Supply2Gov.uk	www.supply2.gov.uk
SIMAP	simap.europa.eu
Official Journal of the European Union (OJEU)	ted.europa.eu
OJEU Reporter	www.ojeu.com
Office of Government Commerce (OGC)	www.ogc.gov.uk

Business services

RIBA Enterprises	www.ribaenterprises.com
NBS	www.thenbs.com
BRE	www.bre.co.uk
BSI	www.bsi-global.com

Claims

County Court Service	www.hmcourts-service.gov.uk or www.moneyclaim.gov.uk

Benchmarking and key performance indicators

Benchmark Index	www.benchmarkindex.com
BSI	www.bsi-emea.com/BenchMark
CBI	www.cbi.org.uk
Colander	www.colander.co.uk
Constructing Excellence	www.constructingexcellence.org.uk or www.kpizone.com
RIBA	www.architecture.com

Employment advice

RIBA Professional Education and Development Resource	www.pedr.co.uk

Government departments/agencies

Cabinet Office	www.cabinetoffice.gov.uk
HM Treasury	www.hm-treasury.gov.uk

Department for Communities and Local Government	www.communities.gov.uk
Department of Trade and Industry	www.dti.gov.uk
Department for Culture, Media and Sport	www.culture.gov.uk
Department for Environment, Food and Rural Affairs	www.defra.gov.uk
Commission for Architecture and the Built Environment (CABE)	www.cabe.org.uk
English Heritage	www.english-heritage.org.uk
Environment Agency	www.environment-agency.gov.uk
Planning Portal	www.planningportal.gov.uk

Index